Justified by

FAITH

Justified by

FAITH

STEPHEN D. NADAULD

DESERET
BOOK

SALT LAKE CITY, UTAH

Library of Congress Cataloging-in-Publication Data

Justified by faith / Stephen D. Nadauld.
   p.   cm.
   Includes index.
   ISBN 1-57345-831-7 (alk. paper)
    1. Church of Jesus Christ of Latter-day Saints—Doctrines.   2. Faith.   3. Justification.
   4. Grace (Theology)   I. Title.
BX8635.3 .N33 2001
234'.7—dc21   2001001802

Printed in the United States of America   18961-6726

10 9 8 7 6 5 4 3 2 1

Therefore being justified by faith, *we have*
peace with God through our Lord Jesus Christ:
By whom also we have access by faith into this
grace *wherein we stand, and rejoice*
in the hope of the glory of God.

ROMANS 5:1–2

Contents

Acknowledgments

I am very grateful to many who have read and commented on early drafts of this manuscript. I especially appreciate the comments of our children, with whom we have discussed these ideas during our family gospel study hours. I have benefited greatly from the input and suggestions of many friends and my colleagues at Brigham Young University. In particular, I would like to thank Craig Merrill, Grant McQueen, and Kaye Hanson. A special thanks to the editors and designers at Deseret Book Company, whose skill and professionalism have brought this project to fruition. Lastly, I would like to thank my wife, Margaret, for her encouragement and strength. Together we have laughed and cried and learned to better love the Lord.

Introduction

The principles of the gospel are a joy to study and understand. Consider, for example, the passage from Paul's epistle to the Romans from which the book takes its title. "Therefore being *justified by faith*, we have peace with God through our Lord Jesus Christ: By whom also we have access by faith into this *grace* wherein we stand, and rejoice in the hope of the glory of God" (Romans 5:1–2; emphasis added). Contained in these verses are three concepts: faith, justification, and grace, whose complete and correct meaning are at the heart of our understanding of the gospel.

I hope in these pages to communicate the elegance of faith, the logic of justification, and the emotion of grace. Their study is important because our gospel understanding is generally framed by certain key concepts, and the correctness of our understanding depends first on our ability to accurately define those concepts and second, to see how they fit into some grand design. Faith, justification, and grace are three significant religious concepts which, when fully defined, add significantly to a knowledge of the plan of redemption and the process of sanctification or cleansing that is fundamental to the plan. The theme that is common to all three concepts is the importance of Jesus Christ and his role in the plan as Savior and Redeemer.

The purpose of this book is to provide definitions of each of these three concepts and to investigate how each functions as part of the process that must act on every individual who wishes to return to the presence of God. Chapters 1 and 2 present an expanded definition of what is meant by religious faith. Chapter 3 takes a somewhat unconventional (at least in religious terms) approach to the discussion of the process of developing faith. Chapter 4 provides a definition of justification, but the major emphasis of the chapter is understanding what is meant by the process of justification and how it works in individual lives. Chapter 5 investigates the multiple meanings of grace and cele-brates the extraordinary blessings inherent in its application.

I'm convinced that an understanding of these topics is a wonderful way to develop a greater appreciation of the role and mission of Jesus Christ. I hope your testimony of the Savior is increased as much by reading these concepts as mine has been by writing them.

1

Faith and ASSURANCES

"Now faith is the substance of things hoped for, the evidence of things not seen."

HEBREWS 11:1

A little boy reached out eagerly to take the string from his father's hand. Attached to the other end of the string was a large balloon that floated in the bright sunshine. As the boy grasped the string, the balloon pulled and tugged at his arm until both his arm and his gaze were extended upward. With one hand held tightly to the string and the other held by his loving father, the delighted boy skipped along the path toward home. The boy did not know the laws of physics that kept the helium-filled balloon floating so gaily in the air. That knowledge would come later. He did know that he'd taken hold of something wonderful given to him by his father. He knew that there was a buoyant lifting force on the other end of the string. Perhaps he imagined that by holding enough balloons he could be lifted off the ground and would float gently into heaven.

Faith is not unlike the unseen power that lifts the balloon. For some, the process of developing faith is as simple as receiving a helium-filled balloon from a parent. But for many others faith is a more difficult and ethereal abstraction. I believe one reason for that difficulty is the lack of a good working definition. When we are asked, "What is faith?" we often struggle to provide a clear definition that allows us to determine whether or not we have it. We can be lifted in reach and gaze by our faith and all the while wonder if we understand the concept.

I wish to write about faith because I believe it is possible to develop a clear definition that can greatly enhance our understanding of this first principle of the gospel. But I also hope to make clear the critical linkage between faith, justification, and the atoning blood of the Savior. Because the logic and linkages are so important, at least at the outset our approach will be more analytical than emotional; we will look at faith as we would look at helium, if you will.

Fortunately, a limited understanding of the physics of helium does not constrain its lifting power. But an improved understanding does enhance one's ability to tap into that lifting power. So it is with faith. The lifting, buoying, saving power of faith in Christ that can be accessed by believing children and believing adults is not constrained by the level of our understanding. Thus I firmly believe that if we will hold to the string of faith and reach out for our Heavenly Father's hand we will be lifted into heaven. But I also believe, and with equal certainty, that improving our understanding of faith will better allow us to tap into its saving power. We will therefore analyze and define faith to better understand it, keeping in mind that the analysis and definition are not the ends but the means.

TWO EXAMPLES

I once met with a very engaging and impressive young couple in their late twenties. She had a bachelor's degree from one of the nation's finest universities. He had a master's degree from the premier institution in his field. They were both raised in the Church, actively attended their church meetings, and willingly accepted church callings. After a few minutes of talking about a variety of subjects, they raised the issue that had motivated their visit. They had been married five years and wanted very much to have children. The young woman seemed especially worried that she hadn't been able to conceive.

We talked for some time about the problem, and then I turned to her and asked if she had ever thought about receiving a priesthood blessing. She replied, "Oh, no, I couldn't do that. What if I received a blessing and then didn't get pregnant? It would destroy my faith!" *Destroy your faith!* I thought to myself. *Isn't that a little dramatic?* Still, I realized she was sincere in her concern.

In time we concluded our visit, but her comment about the impact of a blessing on her faith continued to intrigue me. I wondered what she understood about faith and wished we had had time to further discuss it together. It may be that she did indeed have faith, but it seemed that faith was not a concept she understood well, and consequently she lacked confidence in it. I believe she did not recognize the faith she had, and therefore it served her less well than it might have otherwise.

Contrast that example to the experience of Elder Matthew Cowley as he ministered among the Maori people of New Zealand. He describes the experience this way. "I was asked to administer to a baby in New Zealand. I was able to bless it. The father came up to me with this child, fourteen months old, and he said, 'Our child has not been blessed yet, so I want you to give it a name.' I said, 'All right, what is the name?' He gave me the name of the child, and then he said in a matter-of-fact way, 'While you are giving it its name, give it its sight.' The child was born blind. He said, 'We have had it to the specialists in Wellington. They said it was born blind and they cannot do anything for it. So while you are giving it a name by the same authority you use to give it a name, give it its vision.' Eight months later I saw the child and *it saw me* . . . " (Henry A. Smith, *Matthew Cowley: Man of Faith*, Salt Lake City: Bookcraft, 1954, 138–39).

Should we conclude from these two examples that faith is simply a strong belief, which some are blessed to have and some are not, and that we should not attempt to complicate it any further? Perhaps—but after some thought and study I return again to the notion that analysis of the concept can considerably enhance our understanding of faith as the first and most important principle of the gospel. In turn, that understanding can help us to use faith as an active force to bless our lives. To begin that analysis let us sharpen our focus by considering the issue of semantics—the meaning of words.

There is a difference between faith as a religious principle and the many other uses of the word. For example, a set of tenets or beliefs is sometimes referred to as a person's *faith*. One may keep *faith* with one's supporters, meaning maintaining loyalty or allegiance. Synonyms of faith include *belief* or *trust*. These often connote a generally held or accepted tenet such as having faith that the sun will come up in the morning or that spring will follow winter. While it is useful to understand the many meanings that are currently ascribed to the word *faith*, it is not simply useful but critically important that we understand the meaning of faith in a religious sense. I believe that as we understand faith in more rigorous and well-defined terms, we can then speak more specifically about how to increase and strengthen it. I also believe we gain significant benefits when we come to a better understanding of the role that faith plays in the *process* of redemption.

WHAT IS FAITH?

Each of us—like Adam, Eve, and their children—must come to earth and have the experience of discovering, comprehending, and developing faith, and having it challenged by life's trials and tribulations. For some, like the young woman who feared a blessing, faith may be an ethereal concept that is hard to define. People typically ask, What exactly is faith? How can we know if we have faith? How can we increase our faith? As we better *define* faith, we are better able to recognize it, increase it, and draw upon it as a redeeming principle of the gospel.

The Apostle Paul provides us with a starting point by offering a wonderful definition of faith in his epistle to the Hebrews. This well-known definition is found in the eleventh chapter and reads: "Now faith is the substance of things hoped for, the evidence of things not seen" (Hebrews 11:1). This assertion that faith is a substance or evidence seems at first to run counter to the sense in which the term is generally used. Faith is not usually thought of as a tangible substance to be touched or felt but rather as a feeling or concept—an intangible. Indeed, something accepted on faith often means it is accepted *without* proof, evidence, or substance. So how can faith be substance? Our confusion at considering faith as a substance leads to an interesting and very revealing discovery.

A reading of the footnote in the LDS edition of the Bible explains that an alternative translation of the original Greek could include words such as *assurance, basis,* or *foundation* in place of the word *substance.* The footnote also reveals that in his inspired translation of the Bible, the Prophet Joseph Smith rendered the word *substance* as *assurance.* We find the same reading used in the lectures on faith, which were given in Kirtland, Ohio, during the winter of 1834 to 1835 (see *Lectures on Faith,* 1:1–9). We will see that substituting the word *assurance* for the word *substance* will lessen our confusion and add considerably to our understanding.

A WORKING DEFINITION OF FAITH

Using the insight gained from Joseph Smith's alternative translation, let us proceed to develop an expanded working definition of faith. The basis of our expanded working definition will be the previously quoted verse from Hebrews, "Now faith is the substance of things hoped for, the evidence of things not seen" (Hebrews 11:1). We will begin by replacing the word *substance* with the word *assurance* and then continue by adding several additional words. The first part of the expanded definition becomes:

> **Having faith is *having or accepting* the assurance of things hoped for.**

Note that in the expanded definition I have added the words *Having* and *having or accepting* to accompany the change from *substance* to *assurance*. Since assurances are usually considered to be held or given, the addition of the words *having or accepting* helps convey that meaning.

The second part of the expanded definition then becomes:

> **Having faith is *having or accepting* the evidence of things not seen.**

With that addition, our preliminary definition has become:

> **Having faith is *having or accepting* the assurance of things hoped for, and *having or accepting* the evidence of things not seen.**

Note that by defining faith in terms of assurance and evidence we are not discounting that for some the gift of faith may

7

be its own assurance of the existence of God. We will be in a better position to understand that argument after further enhancements to the definition. With that in mind, we will continue by proposing that both assurances and evidences can be divided into two types.

Assurances may be both (1) mortal and (2) heavenly; and evidences may be both (1) macro and (2) micro. With these additions we come to a completed expanded definition of faith as it is presented in Hebrews:

> *Having* faith is *having or accepting mortal assurances and heavenly assurances* of things hoped for, and *having or accepting macro-*evidence and *microevidence* of things not seen.

In the rest of this chapter we will explore what is meant by "things hoped for" and what these "assurances" consist of. The next chapter will address macro- and microevidences.

THINGS HOPED FOR

Both the original and expanded definitions of faith speak of "things hoped for." Hope is often coupled with faith, as in the well-known phrase "faith, hope, and charity." To hope is to have earnest expectations (Romans 8:19) or to look forward to something with confidence of fulfillment. Throughout the Old and New Testaments we read of the objects of hope: hope in the Lord (Psalms 38:15; Jeremiah 27:7), hope in the resurrection (Acts 23:6), hope in eternal life (Titus 1:2; 3:7), and hope in Christ (1 Corinthians 15:19; 1 Timothy 1:1). Thus, the things ever hoped for or looked forward to with confidence of fulfillment are the reality of Christ, his atonement, his resurrection, and his promise of eternal life.

In the Book of Mormon, Nephi encourages us to "press forward with a steadfastness in Christ, having a perfect brightness of hope" (2 Nephi 31:20). Nephi's brother Jacob observes, "For, for this intent have we written these things, that they may know that we knew of Christ, and we had a hope of his glory many hundred years before his coming; and not only we ourselves had a hope of his glory, but also all the holy prophets which were before us" (Jacob 4:4). Finally, Moroni provides a superb one-verse summary of the things hoped for. He says, "And what is it that ye shall hope for? Behold I say unto you that ye shall have hope through the atonement of Christ and the power of his resurrection, to be raised unto life eternal, and this because of your faith in him according to the promise" (Moroni 7:41).

We see that Old Testament, New Testament, and Book of Mormon prophets all understood that certain elements of the plan under which we all operate could be anticipated with confidence or hope. These things hoped for are the blessings promised to those who agreed to take part in the plan of happiness. They are the blessings of the resurrection, the atonement, and eternal life, which were obtained for us by Jesus Christ, the Son of God. These are the blessings that we look forward to with earnest expectation and with confidence in their fulfillment. These are the objects of our hope, and as such are integral to our definition of what is meant by faith.

ASSURANCES

Having identified the things hoped for, our next step in the understanding of faith is to recognize that our hope is *supported by* assurances. Our expanded definition directs us to the heart of the issue, which is, What is meant by assurances? What is their nature? Although our individual experience may suggest a number of different types, for this discussion we will propose two kinds: mortal assurances and heavenly assurances.

Doctrine and Covenants 46 suggests this same approach. There we read, "To some it is given by the Holy Ghost to know that Jesus Christ is the Son of God, and that he was crucified for the sins of the world. To others it is given to believe on their words, that they also might have eternal life if they continue faithful" (D&C 46:13–14). The phrase "To some it is given to know by the Holy Ghost that Jesus Christ is the Son of God" speaks clearly to the concept of heavenly assurances. Mortal assurances are illustrated by the phrase, "To others it is given to believe on their words." Thus the scripture speaks of heavenly assurances, those that come through the Holy Ghost, and mortal assurances, those that come to us by way of a mortal person.

MORTAL ASSURANCES

Mortal assurances of essential gospel truths are often the starting point for developing individual faith. Mortal assurances may come from parents, religious leaders, or friends as they share their witness or their belief in Christ, and of his atonement, resurrection, and eternal life. This has been true from the beginning of earth's existence. For example, we read, "And

Adam and Eve blessed the name of God, and they made all things known unto their sons and their daughters" (Moses 5:12). In other words, Adam and Eve learned certain truths about Christ and eternal life directly from God (and angels); they then conveyed to their children their assurances of the truth of those things. Parents of every dispensation have had the responsibility to teach of Christ and provide such assurances to their children.

Parents of this last dispensation are strongly counseled: "Inasmuch as parents have children in Zion, or in any of her stakes which are organized, that teach them not . . . faith in Christ the Son of the living God, . . . the sin be upon the heads of the parents" (D&C 68:25).

In a general Young Women meeting address, Sister Sharon Larsen, second counselor in the Young Women general presidency, talked about the assurances she received from her parents. "The testimony of my parents has been a strength to me throughout my life. The first line of their last will and testament describes what they left for their children after their death: 'We leave with you, our children, our testimony that God lives, that Jesus Christ, the Only Begotten in the flesh, also lives.' Their testimonies of faith in the Lord took up most of the first page of their will, and then one simple sentence followed: 'Divide up the material things, and what you don't want give to someone in need or take to the dump.' There wasn't much to divide up, but the wealth of their testimonies made us rich indeed!

"Mom and Dad gave us their most precious possession—their testimonies of the gospel of Jesus Christ, ending with these words: 'May your hearts ever be open and your feelings tender toward these great truths, is our humble prayer'" (*Ensign*, May 2000, 90).

The obligation to provide assurances is not limited only to parents' responsibility to teach eternal truths to their children. In fact, the idea of providing mortal assurances is so important that we have a regular Church meeting whose purpose and design is to provide a setting where mortal assurances can be shared. These monthly fast-and-testimony meetings are unusual both in format and context. Their express purpose is to build faith through sharing assurances. When we bear our testimony we have an opportunity to provide assurances that others might accept. If we wish to *increase the faith* of those present and to be in harmony with the purpose of the meeting, those assurances must be of "things hoped for" identified in the scriptures. Warm personalities, charisma, and travel experiences all have some appointed place, but the basic purpose for a testimony meeting is to stand and add our witness of gospel truths. Can we add our assurance that there is a plan of redemption, a Savior, an atonement, a resurrection, and an eternal life?

I know a young, impetuous, but very loving bishop who, after a testimony meeting approached a youthful member of his ward who had spoken in the meeting. He invited her into his office and said in a way that only he could, "That's an interesting testimony that you bore. Would you be willing to take this Book of Mormon home, read it every day for a month and come back next time and try it again?"

Now I hasten to add that this is not standard operating

procedure. We would never want to risk offending anyone in an area as sensitive as that of personal testimony. But clearly the bishop felt impressed to help the youthful member gain a better understanding of what constituted a testimony. He also hoped to clarify for the individual the purpose of testimony meeting. In this case his loving counsel was received in the spirit in which it was given, the person was motivated, and she returned the next month to strengthen others with a strong witness of "things hoped for."

ALMA AND MORTAL ASSURANCES

Alma understood that assurances from others are often the starting point for the development of faith. Alma 32 describes Alma's teachings to a group of people called Zoramites. Consider these teachings as diagrammed in figure 1. In the diagram, assurances are categorized as mortal or heavenly and are further characterized as already held or as willing to be considered.

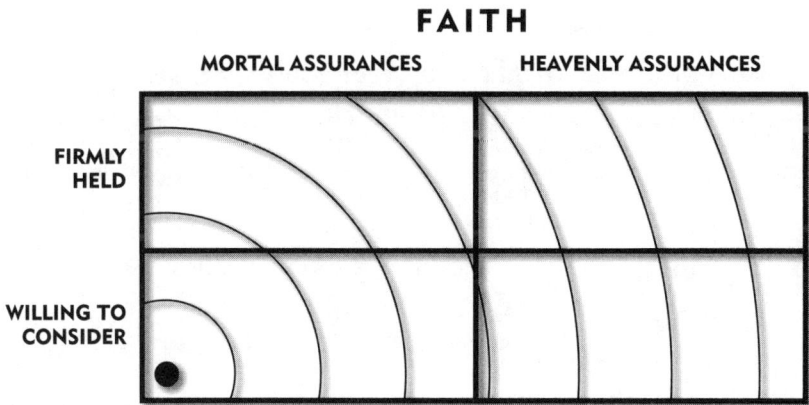

FAITH

MORTAL ASSURANCES	HEAVENLY ASSURANCES

FIRMLY HELD

WILLING TO CONSIDER

Figure 1

Alma was operating with the Zoramites in the lower left-hand corner of the diagram in the box labeled *Willing to Consider—Mortal Assurances*. The small black dot represents the seed spoken of by Alma. Alma begins by explaining that having small assurances does not constitute a complete faith or a perfect knowledge. He observes, "Now, as I said concerning faith—that it was not a perfect knowledge—even so it is with my words. Ye cannot know of their surety at first, unto perfection, any more than faith is a perfect knowledge" (Alma 32:26).

Alma was saying, in essence, "I give you my words or mortal, personal assurances, and you may not immediately accept or believe them." Then he added, "'If ye can no more than desire to believe, let this desire work in you, even until ye believe in a manner that ye can give place for a portion of my words" (v. 27). In other words, just let a portion or small part of my assurances (or words) rest in your heart and mind, and ponder them. Alma compared his first assurances ("portion of my words") to a seed which, if it were good and not cast out by immediate unbelief, would begin to grow. He promised that the growth of the seed would enlarge their souls and enlighten their understanding. Then he observed, "Now behold, would not this increase your faith? I say unto you, Yea; nevertheless it hath not grown up to a perfect knowledge" (v. 29).

As in the diagram, receiving the first assurances (represented by the black dot) constitutes planting the seed. Growth of the seed (represented by the expanding curved lines) is accomplished through the receipt of additional assurances and constitutes an *increase* in faith. Alma recognized there is considerable room for faith to grow through acceptance of additional assurances. He made this point by saying, "Neither must ye lay aside your faith, for ye have only exercised your faith to plant the seed that ye might try the experiment to know if the seed was good. And behold, as the tree beginneth to grow, ye will say: Let us nourish it with great care, that it may get root, that it may grow up, and bring forth fruit unto us. And now behold, if ye nourish it with much care it will get root, and grow up, and bring forth fruit" (vv. 36–37).

Alma says, "Neither must ye lay aside your faith." He makes the point that the initial assurances or planting of the seed must *not* be considered as the finished product to then be laid aside. Planting the seed is a good beginning, but the fruit will come only as the seed is nourished and tended into a tree. So it is with the first small assurances of gospel truths. They must be nourished by seeking and receiving additional assurances and evidences, including, of necessity, the divine assurance provided by the witness of the Holy Ghost.

Finally, Alma points out that the seed shall become a tree springing up unto eternal life. He says of the fruit, "And because of your diligence and your faith and your patience with the word in nourishing it, that it may take root in you, behold, by and by ye shall pluck the fruit thereof, which is most precious, which is sweet above all that is sweet, and which is white above all that is white, yea, and pure above all that is pure; and ye shall feast upon this fruit even until ye are filled, that ye hunger not, neither shall ye thirst" (v. 42).

Alma's experience reminds us that missionary work in every

dispensation relies heavily upon the power of mortal assurances. Even as Alma testified or gave assurances to the Zoramites, so today's missionaries are encouraged to bear their testimony or provide mortal assurance about each gospel principle that is taught. The bearing of testimony not only gives the missionary's personal assurance to an investigator, but it also provides a vehicle for the Holy Ghost to add a heavenly assurance or witness. Missionaries are encouraged to bear testimony at the earliest possible opportunity so that the process of building faith through assurances may have an immediate beginning. The feelings that are thus engendered are described by Alma: "Your understanding doth begin to be enlightened, and your mind doth begin to expand" (v. 34). For many this expanding and enlightening commence as they hear the first words of assurance and testimony proffered by two young missionaries standing on their doorsteps. A willingness to consider these sincere assurances constitutes the inauguration of faith.

FAITH AS A GIFT

Even though faith can be inaugurated with mortal assurances and grow as the seed described by Alma, the scriptures indicate that faith may also begin as a gift. As Moroni taught, "Deny not the gifts of God, for they are many; and they come from the same God. . . . For behold, to one is given by the Spirit of God, that he may teach the word of wisdom; and to another, that he may teach the word of knowledge by the same Spirit; and to another, *exceedingly great faith*; and to another, the gifts of healing by the same Spirit" (Moroni 10:8–11; emphasis added).

Moroni observed that "all these gifts come by the Spirit of Christ; and they come unto every man severally, *according as he will*" (v. 17; emphasis added), and also, "they are given by the manifestations of the Spirit of God unto men, *to profit them*" (v. 8; emphasis added). Spiritual gifts are given according to the will of God with the purpose of profiting men on the earth. Some are blessed with the gift of exceedingly great faith for the benefit of others, whose faith will be increased by listening to the assurances given.

This concept of faith as a gift is also illustrated in previously quoted verses from Doctrine and Covenants 46:

"For all have not every gift given unto them; for there are many gifts, and to every man is given a gift by the Spirit of God. To some is given one, and to some is given another, that all may be profited thereby.

"To some it is given by the Holy Ghost to know that Jesus Christ is the Son of God, and that he was crucified for the sins of the world. To others it is given to believe on their words, that they also might have eternal life if they continue faithful" (D&C 46:11–14).

Verse 11 points out that not all have every gift given unto them. Yes, for some faith begins as a gift. And for them, as noted earlier, the gift is itself an assurance or an evidence. But for many the process begins by accepting the personal assurances or believing on the words of others and then "nurturing the seed" as described by Alma.

It is clear that salvation is not restricted only to those who have faith as an inborn or ready gift. Verse 14 teaches that eternal life is also readily available to those who allow their faith to be inaugurated by the words or assurances given by others.

FAITH IN EACH STAGE OF EXISTENCE

It is interesting to note that the need for faith extends beyond the bounds of this mortal existence. That this is the case can be understood by reading from Alma 13.

"And I would that ye should remember that the Lord God ordained priests after his holy order, which was after the order of his Son, to teach these things unto the people. And those priests were ordained after the order of his Son, in a manner that thereby the people might know in what manner to look forward to his Son for redemption.

"And this is the manner after which they were ordained—being called and prepared from the foundation of the world according to the foreknowledge of God, on account of *their exceeding faith* and good works; in the first place being left to choose good or evil; therefore they having chosen good, and exercising *exceedingly great faith*, are called with a holy calling, yea, with that holy calling which was prepared with, and according to, a preparatory redemption for such" (Alma 13:1–3; emphasis added).

This scripture states that priests were called and prepared according to the foreknowledge of God, on account of "their exceeding faith." That faith is then referred to as "exceedingly great faith." It seems clear that God knew his children in premortality and observed some of them exhibiting markedly greater faith than others. Some suppose that faith is a concept that relates only to this earthly existence and is required of men and women here because there is a veil between us and our contact with God. They surmise that without that veil they would not need to exercise faith in things not seen, because all would be open to our view.

However, these verses in Alma make it clear that faith was a trait exhibited by valiant spirits in the premortal existence. Upon reflection we realize that our faith—even in the premortal existence—must have been focused on Christ and the plan of redemption proposed by the Father and the Son. While we may have had an intimate knowledge of the plan, it was still simply a plan, *not yet a reality*. We had to believe the plan would actually work. We had to believe that Jesus would really come to earth as a helpless infant, would live a perfect life, would withstand the temptations of the devil, and ultimately not shrink from partaking of the bitter cup of suffering in Gethsemane and the crucifixion on Calvary.

Our willingness to believe was undoubtedly bolstered as we shared our assurances with one another. So even then, as now, faith seems to have consisted of accepting assurances of things hoped for but not seen. An advantage we have from our current perspective (if we choose to let it be an advantage) is that we now have a record that some of the elements of the plan have already transpired. For example, we have two written records, the Bible and the Book of Mormon, that witness of the birth, atonement, and resurrection of Jesus Christ.

Our position in the premortal existence relative to faith was not unlike that experienced by the Nephites and expressed by Jacob, the brother of Nephi: "For, for this intent have we written these things, that they may know that we *knew of Christ*, and we had a hope of his glory *many hundred years before his coming*; and not only we ourselves had a hope of his glory, but also all the holy prophets which were before us" (Jacob 4:4; emphasis added).

Our expression of faith during the premortal existence must have been like that described by Jacob. We knew of Christ and had a hope of his glory many hundreds, indeed thousands, of years before his coming—or *our* coming.

The scriptures also point out that faith will be a principle that will continue to operate *after* men are dead. President Joseph F. Smith recorded in Doctrine and Covenants 138: "And as I wondered, my eyes were opened, and my understanding quickened, and I perceived that the Lord *went not in person* among the wicked and the disobedient who had rejected the truth, to teach them; but behold, from among the righteous, he organized his forces and appointed messengers, clothed with power and authority, and commissioned them to go forth and carry the light of the gospel to them that were in darkness, even to all the spirits of men; and thus was the gospel preached to the dead. . . .

"These were taught *faith* in God, repentance from sin, vicarious baptism for the remission of sins, the gift of the Holy

Ghost by the laying on of hands" (D&C 138:29–30, 33; emphasis added).

These verses illustrate that even after men are dead faith will be an operative principle. Isn't it interesting to note that because the Lord will not go in person to the wicked, the teaching of faith in the hereafter will be very similar to our experience on earth. The teaching will begin with the proffering of assurances by "appointed messengers, clothed with power and authority."

ASSURANCES FROM MODERN PROPHETS AND APOSTLES

One of the great blessings of living in these latter days, when the gospel has been restored, is that we have the opportunity to be given assurances of eternal things by living prophets and apostles. Modern mass communication makes it possible for appointed messengers to bear witness of Christ and his atonement, resurrection, and promise of eternal life to millions throughout the earth. Providing assurances of these truths is one of the essential functions of semiannual general conferences and is why each of the fifteen men sustained as prophets, seers, and revelators speaks at least once during the conference proceedings.

Indeed, apostles and prophets providing assurance of things hoped for is the basis of one of the most powerful declarations of our day. The declaration titled "The Living Christ," dated 1 January 2000, contains the testimony of the apostles of Jesus Christ to all the world. The final paragraph reads, "We bear testimony, as His duly ordained Apostles—that Jesus is the Living

Christ, the immortal Son of God. He is the great King Immanuel, who stands today on the right hand of His Father. He is the light, the life, and the hope of the world. His way is the path that leads to happiness in this life and eternal life in the world to come. God be thanked for the matchless gift of His divine Son." To the document are appended the signatures of fifteen modern prophets and apostles, each of whom desires that his assurance of the divinity of Christ be accepted by all who seek to know the truth.

In addition to apostles and prophets, we have local priesthood and sister leaders from whom we can receive assurances of the divine nature of Christ and the reality of his ministry. Parents, family members, and friends add to the fabric and texture of our mortal-assurance tapestry. Surely one very important aspect of having faith is receiving or accepting *mortal assurances* of those blessings we hope for most: forgiveness through the atonement, resurrection of our physical bodies, and eternal life with our Heavenly Father.

HEAVENLY ASSURANCES

We now turn our attention to heavenly assurances. Alma 12 provides a very interesting insight into the need for heavenly assurances. He begins by introducing the concept of the plan of redemption (Alma 12:25) and then makes this observation: "After God had appointed that these things [the plan of redemption] should come unto man, behold, then he saw that it was expedient that man should know concerning the things whereof he had appointed unto them" (v. 28).

From this scripture we learn that God ordained a plan of redemption for his children and also recognized the need to communicate with them and provide information concerning that plan and to give assurances of its promised blessings. Alma further points out, "Therefore *he sent angels to converse* with them, who caused men to behold of his glory. And they began from that time forth to call on his name; therefore God *conversed* with men, and made known unto them the plan of redemption, which had been prepared from the foundation of the world" (vv. 29–30; emphasis added).

Alma observed, then, that heavenly communication comes from angels as well as from God himself.

Mormon, in his great discourse on faith (as recorded by his son, Moroni), speaks of the role that heavenly assurances play in the development of faith. He begins by saying, "And now I come to that faith, of which I said I would speak." He then pointed out that "God . . . sent angels to minister unto the children of men, to make manifest concerning the coming of Christ; and God also declared unto prophets, by his own mouth, that Christ should come" (Moroni 7:21–23).

Mormon commences his discourse on faith by instructing his brethren that God both personally and through his appointed heavenly messengers (angels) provided assurances that Christ would come. These heavenly assurances established a basis upon which men could begin to exercise their faith in Christ. "Wherefore, by the ministering of angels, and by every word which proceeded forth out of the mouth of God, men *began to exercise faith* in Christ" (v. 25; emphasis added).

In continuing to make his point about heavenly assurances, Mormon added some instruction about the "office" of angels. "For behold, they [angels] are subject unto him, to minister according to the word of his command. . . . And the office of their ministry is to call men unto repentance, and to fulfill and to do the work of the covenants of the Father, which he hath made unto the children of men, to prepare the way among the children of men, *by declaring the word of Christ unto the chosen vessels of the Lord, that they may bear testimony of him*" (vv. 30–31; emphasis added).

The duties of those who hold the office of angel are (1) to call men unto repentance, (2) to fulfill and do the work of the covenants of the Father, and (3) to prepare the way by declaring the word of Christ unto the chosen vessels of the Lord. (Mormon's son, Moroni, must have listened carefully to his father's teachings on the office of angels because he perfectly exemplified the duties of that office during his angelic ministry to the Prophet Joseph Smith.)

Mormon's explanation as to why angels provide heavenly assurances to some individuals is found in the last part of verse 31. He states that heavenly assurances of Christ are provided "unto the chosen vessels of the Lord, that they may bear testimony of him." If Mormon had ended here we could correctly infer from the phrase "that they may bear testimony of him" that prophets, having received heavenly assurances, would then bear testimony or provide assurances to others. However, Mormon chooses to make that point explicitly, for in the very next verse we read, "And by so doing, the Lord God prepareth the way that the residue of men may have faith in Christ, that the Holy Ghost may have place in their hearts [by having chosen vessels bear testimony], according to the power thereof; and after this manner bringeth to pass the Father, the covenants which he hath made unto the children of men" (v. 32). Mormon explains that the act of chosen vessels bearing testimony not only provides the mortal assurances upon which the rest of us can begin our faith but also prepares our hearts for the Holy Ghost to bear witness and to provide to each individual a heavenly assurance of the reality of Christ and his divine mission.

These teachings about the receipt of heavenly assurances were clearly understood by the Prophet Joseph Smith. Doctrine and Covenants 20 describes how communication comes from heaven: "And we know that these things are true and according to the revelations of John, neither adding to, nor diminishing from the prophecy of his book, the holy scriptures, or the revelations of God which shall come hereafter *by the gift and power of the Holy Ghost, the voice of God, or the ministering of angels*" (D&C 20:35; emphasis added).

This verse confirms that heavenly communication or assurances may come from three possible sources, the Holy Ghost, the voice of God, or the ministering of angels.

ADAM AND HEAVENLY ASSURANCES

Adam was blessed to receive heavenly assurances in each of the three possible ways. Consider again from the book of Moses the account of Adam's experience after being cast out of the Garden of Eden. The first heavenly communication came from the voice of the Lord: "And they *heard the voice of the Lord* from the way toward the Garden of Eden, speaking unto them. . . . And he gave unto them commandments, that they should worship the Lord their God, and should offer the firstlings of their flocks, for an offering unto the Lord" (Moses 5:4–5; emphasis added).

Next Adam and Eve were visited by an angel: "And after many days *an angel of the Lord appeared unto Adam*, saying: Why dost thou offer sacrifices unto the Lord? And Adam said unto him: I know not, save the Lord commanded me.

"And then the angel spake, saying: This thing is a similitude of the sacrifice of the Only Begotten of the Father, which is full of grace and truth. Wherefore, thou shalt do all that thou doest in the name of the Son, and thou shalt repent and call upon God in the name of the Son forevermore" (Moses 4:6–8; emphasis added).

And finally came the witness of the Holy Ghost: "And in that day *the Holy Ghost fell upon Adam*, which beareth record of the Father and the Son, saying: I am the Only Begotten of the Father from the beginning, henceforth and forever, that as thou hast fallen thou mayest be redeemed, and all mankind, even as many as will" (Moses 5:9; emphasis added).

As the first man on the earth, Adam could not have received assurances of the kind that we have categorized as mortal. Because there were no other human beings, Adam's first assurances had to be of the heavenly type. We may wonder why all three kinds of heavenly assurances were needed. Many of us might conclude that a simple personal visit from an angel would be quite a nice assurance! Do we suppose that Adam and Eve needed extra assurance or special convincing? I think not. Adam was very clearly one who had exhibited exceedingly great faith in the premortal existence. He was one of the gods involved in the creation and one of the Father's most valiant spirits (Abraham 3:22–23). His was not a spirit that needed remedial attention.

God's visit to Adam constituted the opening of the first dispensation of the gospel upon the earth. We know God's work and glory is "to bring to pass the immortality and eternal life of man" (Moses 1:39). Beginning his work on earth with a personal visit to Adam is exactly what we would expect. The angel's visit constituted a continuation of instruction concerning sacrifice, repentance, and prayer. But what about the witness of the Holy Ghost. Why would it be needed as well?

It was essential that Adam receive a witness of the Holy Ghost for at least two reasons. First, the Holy Ghost has an official or ordained role as a testator or witness. It would be important to begin the first dispensation of the gospel with the Holy Ghost fulfilling his officially constituted assignment. Second, Adam would need to be a teacher to his children and many succeeding generations. His personal experience with the Holy Ghost would allow him to teach others of its testifying power. In addition, we know from the scriptural record that heavenly visitations do not always result in conversion. The experience of Nephi's brothers, Laman and Lemuel, is a notable example. They had numerous angelic visits and yet remained unwilling to accept the principles they were taught.

JOSEPH SMITH AND HEAVENLY ASSURANCES

To open the *first* dispensation of the gospel upon the earth, heavenly assurances of the things hoped for were given to Adam through the voice of God, the ministering of angels, and the power of the Holy Ghost. When the *last* dispensation was opened, heavenly assurances were given to the Prophet Joseph Smith in exactly the same three ways. Joseph records in his history that this last dispensation was opened by the voice of God:

"When the light rested upon me I saw two Personages, whose brightness and glory defy all description, standing above me in the air. One of them spake unto me, calling me by name and said, pointing to the other—*This is my Beloved Son. Hear Him!*" (Joseph Smith—History 1:17).

The Father introduced the Son and provided indisputable heavenly assurance of his reality and his divine nature as God's Beloved Son. The Father's injunction to "*Hear Him*" pointed the Prophet toward Christ as one whose instruction would be essential to the Prophet's eternal welfare.

Once the voice of God had been heard and the last dispensation was begun, the Prophet Joseph received further assurances through the ministering of angels. He notes in his history that "while I was thus in the act of calling upon God, I discovered a light appearing in my room, which continued to increase until the room was lighter than at noonday, when immediately a personage appeared at my bedside, standing in the air, for his feet did not touch the floor. . . . He called me by name, and said unto me that he was a messenger sent from the presence of God to me, and that his name was Moroni" (vv. 30, 33). In addition to his instruction concerning the Book of Mormon, Moroni quoted scriptures expounding the mission of the Savior. He quoted from Malachi, Isaiah, Acts, and Joel, as well as many other passages of scripture (vv. 36–41).

Perhaps a verse quoted by Moroni from Joel represents the spirit of Moroni's ministering: "And it shall come to pass, that whosoever shall call on the name of the Lord shall be delivered: for in mount Zion and in Jerusalem shall be deliverance, as the Lord hath said, and in the remnant whom the Lord shall call" (Joel 2:32). Through this scripture, Moroni instructed Joseph that deliverance would come by calling on the name of the Lord and that he, Joseph, could be *assured* that the promises contained in the scriptures would be fulfilled.

Many other heavenly messengers were sent to the Prophet with instructions and assurances. One such angelic minister was John the Baptist. Concerning his visit the Prophet writes, "The messenger who visited us on this occasion and conferred this Priesthood upon us, said that his name was John, the same that is called John the Baptist in the New Testament" (Joseph Smith—History 1:72). The purpose of John's visit was to restore the Aaronic Priesthood, giving the Prophet and Oliver Cowdery the power to baptize.

Joseph continued the description of their experience in these words, "Immediately on our coming up out of the water after we had been baptized, we experienced great and glorious blessings from our Heavenly Father. No sooner had I baptized Oliver Cowdery, than the *Holy Ghost* fell upon him, and he stood up and prophesied many things which should shortly come to pass. And again, so soon as I had been baptized by him, I also had the spirit of prophecy, when, standing up, I prophesied concerning the rise of this Church, and many other things connected with the Church, and this generation of the children of men. We were filled with the *Holy Ghost,* and rejoiced in the God of our salvation" (v. 73; emphasis added).

Joseph and Oliver each received a witness from the Holy Ghost concerning the divine nature of the work in which they were engaged. Joseph had heard the voice of the Lord, had experienced the ministering of angels, and now had received heavenly assurances from the Holy Ghost concerning his salvation. With such witnesses and as the prophet of this last dispensation, Joseph was able to extend his assurances to each of us that our faith in the things hoped for might also lead to our salvation.

It is wonderfully reassuring to realize that God opened this last dispensation by providing to a prophet the same heavenly assurances as were provided for the opening of the first dispensation. That such assurances have been renewed in our time is truly an anchor to our faith. It is equally reassuring to acknowledge that our faith can also be strengthened by individual heavenly assurances received from the Holy Ghost. We need not be prophets to enjoy sufficient faith to enable us to return to our Father's presence.

MORTAL AND HEAVENLY ASSURANCES COMBINED

For the sake of analysis we have chosen to partition assurances into the two categories of mortal assurances and heavenly assurances. But we need to emphasize that often mortal and heavenly assurances are manifest simultaneously in the same experience. Because the role of the Holy Ghost is to testify of the divinity of the Savior, when we bear testimony or express our assurance concerning Christ, that expression is often accompanied by the *reassuring* or *reinforcing* influence of the Holy Ghost. The Holy Ghost bears witness or whispers to those who hear us that the words we have spoken are true.

The Holy Ghost uses the spoken word as a vehicle or conveyor for the fulfilling of his mandate to testify of the Savior. Thus, at the same time the words are conveyed into our minds by the speaker, the truthfulness of those words is conveyed into our hearts by the Holy Ghost.

This heavenly assurance from the Holy Ghost may certainly be thought of as a gift. A heavenly assurance cannot be demanded but it may be eagerly sought after. Indeed, we are counseled to "seek . . . earnestly the best gifts" (D&C 46:8). What better gift could be obtained from our earnest petitioning than a heavenly assurance that Jesus Christ is our Savior and Redeemer?

The power of the combination of mortal and heavenly assurances is illustrated by the example of Peter on the day of Pentecost. Elder Dennis B. Neuenschwander observes, "The fundamental responsibility of prophets, seers, and revelators, all of whom bear apostolic authority, is to bear certain testimony of the name of Jesus Christ in all the world. . . . This testimony, borne of the Holy Ghost through revelation, was the heart of the New Testament Church and is the heart of the Church today. On the day of Pentecost, Peter bore pure testimony that

Jesus of Nazareth was 'taken, . . . crucified and slain' and that He was 'raised up, having loosed the pains of death,' of which they, the Apostles were all witnesses. So powerful was this testimony of Jesus Christ, spoken by a living Apostle, that hearts were changed and about 3,000 people were baptized for the remission of their sins" (*Ensign*, Nov. 2000, 40).

The combination of mortal assurances from an authorized servant with heavenly reassurance from the Holy Ghost produced a dramatic result. It can be argued that the same mechanism of combined mortal and heavenly assurances has produced and will continue to produce no less dramatic results in this dispensation of the fulness of the gospel.

In this chapter we've developed an expanded definition of faith as defined in Hebrews 11:1. The expanded definition to this point may be given as:

> **Faith is having or accepting mortal assurances from priesthood leaders, family members, and friends, and heavenly assurances from the Holy Ghost, that Christ lived, atoned for our sins, was resurrected, and promises eternal life.**

2

$\mathcal{F}aith$ and
EVIDENCE

"In this ye have sinned, for ye have rejected all these things,
notwithstanding so many evidences which ye have received."

HELAMAN 8:24

J ason lives across the street. I've been watching him grow
since he was ten years old. He was always far bigger than
any other boy his age and ended up playing tackle on two
great high school football teams. Jason's father, Mike, and I
loved loading our boys up for camping, bicycling, fishing, or any
other activity that fathers and sons could enjoy together. Just
before Mike died of cancer, we sat together on the bank of a beautiful little stream and talked about fishing and boys and heaven.

Last week Jason spoke in his missionary farewell and told a
very simple but insightful story. He described a trip he took with
friends to Hawaii. He talked of water and waves, of sun and
sand and nightlife activities available along the beach. One
night, near the end of their trip, Jason and his friends were

sitting in the lobby of their hotel when a group of girls their age came in from an evening on the town. They began conversing and asking each other questions about where they were from, if they were having a good time, and so forth. Upon learning that the boys were from Utah, the girls inquired if they were "Mormons." The boys affirmed that they were. The conversation continued for a few minutes, but one by one the girls drifted off to their rooms until there were only two left. As soon as the other girls were gone, the remaining two began to ask a series of questions that Jason felt could best be answered from the scriptures. He excused himself for a moment, went to his room to get his Book of Mormon, and returned to rejoin the discussion. After more than an hour of answering questions, Jason fervently bore his testimony that what the girls had been hearing was true. He then handed them the Book of Mormon. He said, "I left them with evidence in their heart and evidence in their hands that the principles we had taught them were true."

Not only is faith about assurances, but it is also about evidence. In this chapter we will be discussing the nature of evidence and the relationship between evidence and faith.

As we saw in chapter 1, part of our expanded definition of faith reads:

> **Having faith is having or accepting the evidence of things not seen.**

Modifying Paul's definition by adding the words *having* and *having or accepting* calls attention to the notion that faith is *not* evidence but rather the act of *accepting* evidence. It is not uncommon to accept evidence of things unseen. For example, we accept a falling apple as evidence of the unseen force of gravity. Broken twigs and imprints in the ground are evidence that an animal, as yet unseen, has nevertheless passed by. Legal proceedings rely heavily on the use of evidence to demonstrate or prove that something unseen by jury members did in fact take place.

Paul understood the nature of evidence, as we can see in Hebrews 11. After stating that "faith is . . . the evidence of things not seen" (Hebrews 11:1), Paul explains in verse three, "Through faith we understand that the worlds were framed by the word of God, so that things which are seen were not made of things which do appear." While in this translation the wording may seem awkward, Paul is simply affirming that the worlds that are seen can be taken as *evidence* of the word of God, which is unseen. Thus the restatement, "*Having* faith is *accepting* evidence of things not seen" is consistent with Paul's example, in which we are encouraged to accept the existence of the world as evidence of the unseen word of God, which created the world.

In the same manner that we have analyzed different kinds of assurances, it is also possible to ponder the possibility of different types of evidence. There are, no doubt, a number of ways that evidence might be classified or typed, but it is sufficient for the current purpose to divide evidence into two broad categories—*macro* and *micro* or, in other words, large and small. These terms are often used in the field of economics. Macroeconomics considers data, principles, or trends that could have an impact on everyone in the economy. Microeconomics is the study of principles that affect individuals or individual business entities. In the same manner, we will define macro, or large, evidence as evidence that is available to everyone and micro, or small, evidence as that which is individual or of a personal nature.

MACROEVIDENCE

There is much that could be categorized as macroevidence of things unseen. Paul's reference to earth and heavens would certainly be considered to be a kind of macro or very large evidence. Macroevidence could also include the scriptures. In addition, there is a category of macroevidence that might best be thought of as "event" evidence. We will consider the creation of the world, the scriptures, and event evidence each in turn.

GOD'S CREATIONS AS MACROEVIDENCE

I agree with Paul that the earth, the seas, the mountains, the streams, and the glorious world we live in are all rich visual evidence of God's unseen hand. My favorite expression of this macroevidence is found in the words of this hymn:

> O Lord my God, when I in awesome wonder
> Consider all the worlds* thy hands have made,
> I see the stars, I hear the rolling* thunder,
> Thy pow'r thruout the universe displayed; . . .

---

*Author's original words are "works" and "mighty."

When thru the woods and forest glades I wander,
And hear the birds sing sweetly in the trees,
When I look down from lofty mountain grandeur
And hear the brook and feel the gentle breeze,

Then sings my soul, my Savior God, to thee,
How great thou art! How great thou art!

Then sings my soul, my Savior God, to thee,
How great thou art! How great thou art!
(*Hymns*, no. 86.)*

Other observers of the heavens and earth have responded in a similar manner. Consider Moses' experience with being shown the handiwork of God and his reaction to it:

"And God spake unto Moses, saying: Behold, I am the Lord God Almighty, and Endless is my name; for I am without beginning of days or end of years; and is not this endless? And, behold, thou art my son; wherefore look, and I will show thee the workmanship of mine hands; but not all, for my works are without end, and also my words, for they never cease. . . .

"And it came to pass that Moses looked, and beheld the world upon which he was created; and Moses beheld the world and the ends thereof, and all the children of men which are, and which were created; of the same he greatly *marveled and wondered*" (Moses 1:3–4, 8; emphasis added).

It appears that Moses was given an astronaut's view of the

---

*Copyright © 1953 S. K. Hine. Assigned to Manna Music, Inc., 35255 Brooten Road, Pacific City, OR 97135. Renewed 1981. All Rights Reserved. Used by permission.

earth as he "beheld the world upon which he was created." He was told specifically that he was seeing the workmanship of God's hands, and the result was that "he greatly marveled and wondered."

Abraham's experience was not unlike that of Moses:

"Thus I, Abraham, talked with the Lord, face to face, as one man talketh with another, and he told me of the works which his hands had made; and he said unto me: My son, my son (and his hand was stretched out), behold I will show you all these. And he put his hand upon mine eyes, and I saw those things which his hands had made, which were many; and they multiplied before mine eyes, and I could not see the end thereof" (Abraham 3:11–12).

Moses and Abraham were each allowed to see the majesty of God's creations in firsthand experiences that left no doubt that the earth and heavens were solid, believable evidence of his existence and power. Many of us, having had a much less dramatic presentation, come to the same conclusion after considering the beauty, intricacy, and harmony of our physical surroundings.

WHAT OF CONTRARY "EVIDENCE"?

Of course, not all observers examine the evidence and render the same judgment. In particular, we sometimes worry about the opinions of members of the scientific community.

Part of the problem lies in differences of training and mindset. It is possible for those not trained in scientific methods to misinterpret both the motives and findings of scientific research;

in the same way, it is possible for the scientist to be critical of the motives and understandings of the believer.

Gerald L. Schroeder, a physicist educated at the Massachusetts Institute of Technology, observes, "Two very different types of researchers toil at understanding our cosmic history. One delves into the secrets of the universe through physics and cosmology. The other relies on interpretations of the Bible. In spite of their common goal, they use such different sources of information that they often appear to be mutually antagonistic. I strongly believe that the antagonism experienced by these two groups is unnecessary" (*Genesis and the Big Bang*, New York: Bantam Books, 1990, 9–10).

I believe most thoughtful scientists agree with Dr. Schroeder that nothing is to be gained by pitting science against religion. The history of science is replete with examples of theories supported by data that endure only long enough for new or different data to spawn replacement theories. Theories of evolution, relativity, quantum mechanics, the big bang, and whatever scientists have had to say about God as Creator all fit into the same category. They can be useful for dealing with some scientific problems but do not provide any reasoned observer with evidence that God is not the creator of man and the universe he inhabits.

A second quotation from Dr. Schroeder makes this point nicely: "For decades, many scientists have prescribed the misconception that there are rational explanations for the origin of the universe, life and mankind. The shortcomings of the popular theories were merely swept under the rug to avoid confusing the issues. The knowledge that scientists do not have these explanations has now been coupled by the awareness of the fossil record's failure to confirm Darwin's (or any other) theory of the gradual evolution of life. The demonstration of the misconceptions has brought many scientists and lay persons to an uncomfortable realization: The problems of our origins, problems that most of us would have preferred to consider solved by experts who should know the answers, in fact have not been solved and are not about to be solved, at least not by the purely scientific methods used to date" (*Genesis and the Big Bang*, 25).

In other words, science has not provided evidence that contradicts the knowledge given to Moses and Abraham that the earth and heavens were created by God. We can believe the prophets, the scriptures, and our own observations and stand in "awesome wonder" at the magnificence of God's creations and clear evidence of his handiwork.

THE SCRIPTURES AS MACROEVIDENCE

I believe the scriptures also serve as extraordinary macroevidence of "things unseen" because they are available to everyone. The Book of Mormon especially is compelling, hold-in-your-hand, read-and-study evidence, just the kind that Paul had in mind. The four standard works together—the Bible, the Book of Mormon, the Doctrine and Covenants, and the Pearl of Great Price—can present to the serious student a body of evidence that has overwhelming power to convince.

THE BIBLE AS MACROEVIDENCE

I like very much what Elder Bruce R. McConkie says of the Bible: "The Bible is a book of books. It has enlightened and influenced the Christian world generally as no other book has ever done. Such measure of truth as was preserved in its pages (as soon as this truth became known to people generally) was instrumental in bringing to pass the Renaissance and of laying the foundation for the restoration of the gospel. When the Bible is read under the guidance of the Spirit, and in harmony with the many latter-day revelations which interpret and make plain its more mysterious parts, it becomes one of the most priceless volumes known to man. 'He who reads it oftenest will like it best, and he who is acquainted with it, will know the Hand [of the Lord] wherever he can see it,' the Prophet taught. (*Teachings*, p. 56.)" (*Mormon Doctrine*, 82–83.)

As "one of the most priceless volumes known to man," the Bible's enormous value lies in the evidence it provides of the doctrines of Christ and his birth, perfect life, atonement, resurrection, and promise of eternal life.

This kind of evidence was considered so important that its acquisition in the form of the brass plates is the basis of one of the most well-known episodes in the Book of Mormon (1 Nephi 3–5). Of the importance of the brass plates Nephi says, "And behold, it is wisdom in God that we should obtain these records, that we may preserve unto our children the language of our fathers; and also that we may preserve unto them the words which have been spoken by the mouth of all the holy prophets, which have been delivered unto them by the Spirit and power of God, since the world began, even down unto this present time" (1 Nephi 3:19–20).

The evidence contained on the plates was of such importance that to obtain the record Nephi was commanded to kill Laban, for "behold the Lord slayeth the wicked to bring forth his righteous purposes. It is better that one man should perish than that a nation should dwindle and perish in unbelief" (1 Nephi 4:13).

Referring to the same plates, Alma explains to his son Helaman, "It has hitherto been wisdom in God that these things should be preserved; for behold, they have enlarged the memory of this people, yea, and convinced many of the error of their ways, and brought them to the knowledge of their God unto the salvation of their souls. . . . These records and their words brought them unto repentance; that is, they brought them to the knowledge of the Lord their God, and to rejoice in Jesus Christ their Redeemer" (Alma 37:8, 9).

The Bible, as macroevidence, can accomplish the same purposes today. It can enlarge our memories, convince us of our errors, teach us of God, and help us rejoice in Jesus Christ our Redeemer.

LATTER-DAY SCRIPTURES AS MACROEVIDENCE

When we consider macroevidence, we should also realize that Latter-day Saints have been given "large" evidence of a most extraordinary sort. That evidence is, of course, the Book of Mormon.

The title page of the Book of Mormon states explicitly that

its purpose is "the convincing of the Jew and Gentile that Jesus is the Christ, the Eternal God." In other words, the very purpose of the Book of Mormon is to *be* the kind of evidence that our definition calls for, the kind of evidence that increases faith in the Lord Jesus Christ and in his promises.

The impact that the Book of Mormon has had, and continues to have, in the development of faith is incalculable. It has been a primary source of evidence for millions who have read it and accepted Moroni's admonition to inquire of the Lord as to its truthfulness. The fact that its translation was accomplished by the gift and power of God is accepted by those who thoughtfully ponder its pages. None of its critics has produced credible evidence that the book is not what it purports to be: an ancient record of God's dealings with a covenant branch of the house of Israel. On the contrary, each year brings additional thousands of people who can newly testify that the Book of Mormon is indeed legitimate evidence from God.

Some seek to prove the Book of Mormon through cultural, linguistic, geographical, or other external evidence. But more important than any scientific evidence, particularly with respect to the development of faith, are the doctrinal principles revealed in its pages. The hoped-for blessings of the atonement and resurrection wrought by Christ are nowhere more clearly testified to than by the Book of Mormon prophets. The beautifully chronicled visit of the Savior to his other sheep constitutes one of the most tender and powerful passages in all of scripture. Truly, the Book of Mormon is macroevidence for any who would investigate without bias.

Of nearly equal stature in the category of macroevidence are the Doctrine and Covenants and the Pearl of Great Price. These two works, together with the Book of Mormon, contribute evidence of the restoration of eternal truths in this last dispensation of the fulness of times. The strength of the scriptural macroevidence is there to be weighed and measured by anyone wishing to be blessed by the increased faith that such examination will produce.

EVENT EVIDENCE

To the macroevidence of the creation and the scriptures can be added the category labeled *event evidence*. It is fascinating to observe how the Book of Mormon prophets used a history of past events as faith-promoting evidence to their people. Nephi, the son of Lehi, understood the link between event evidence and faith and was especially adept at its use. For example, as Nephi and his brothers were returning to the wilderness after having persuaded the family of Ishmael to accompany them, Nephi said to those who were rebelling and wanting to return to Jerusalem, "How is it that ye have not hearkened unto the word of the Lord? How is it that ye have forgotten that ye have seen an angel of the Lord? Yea, and how is it that ye have forgotten what great things the Lord hath done for us, in delivering us out of the hands of Laban, and also that we should obtain this record?" (1 Nephi 7:9–11).

Nephi reminded his brethren of three events of the recent past: the visit of an angel, deliverance from Laban, and the obtaining of the record. He then applied this evidence to faith:

"Yea, and how is it that ye have forgotten that the Lord is able to do all things according to his will, for the children of men, if it so be that they exercise faith in him? Wherefore, let us be faithful to him. And if it so be that we are faithful to him, we shall obtain the land of promise" (1 Nephi 7:12–13).

Nephi resorted again to the recitation of event evidence when he began to build a ship. His account begins: "And when my brethren saw that I was about to build a ship, they began to murmur against me, saying: Our brother is a fool, . . . for they did not believe that I could build a ship; neither would they believe that I was instructed of the Lord" (1 Nephi 17:17–18).

Nephi's brethren continued in a bitter diatribe. When they had concluded, Nephi attempted to restore their faith with a compelling account of remarkable event evidence from their religious tradition: "And it came to pass that I, Nephi, spake unto them, saying: Do ye believe that our fathers, who were the children of Israel, would have been led away out of the hands of the Egyptians if they had not hearkened unto the words of the Lord? . . .

"Now ye know that Moses was commanded of the Lord to do that great work; and ye know that by his word the waters of the Red Sea were divided hither and thither, and they passed through on dry ground. But ye know that the Egyptians were drowned in the Red Sea, who were the armies of Pharaoh. And ye also know that they were fed with manna in the wilderness. Yea, and ye also know that Moses, by his word according to the power of God which was in him, smote the rock, and there came forth water, that the children of Israel might quench their thirst. . . .

"And after they had crossed the river Jordan he did make them mighty unto the driving out of the children of the land, yea, unto the scattering them to destruction" (1 Nephi 17:23, 26–29, 32).

Nephi cited the parting of the Red Sea, the drowning of the Egyptian army, the feeding with manna, the bringing forth of water from a rock, and the securing of the promised land as event evidence he hoped would strengthen the faith of his brothers.

The prophet Alma also understood the use of event evidence. In a stirring testimony to his son Helaman, Alma recites event evidence that sustained and supported him in his faith: "And I know that he will raise me up at the last day, to dwell with him in glory; yea, and I will praise him forever, for he has brought our fathers out of Egypt, . . . and he led them by his power into the promised land; yea, and he has delivered them out of bondage and captivity from time to time. Yea, and he has also brought our fathers out of the land of Jerusalem; and he has also, by his everlasting power, delivered them out of bondage and captivity, from time to time even down to the present day; and I have always retained in remembrance their captivity; yea, and ye also ought to retain in remembrance, as I have done, their captivity" (Alma 36:28–29).

Nephi, the son of Helaman, found himself in the difficult position of having to defend himself when corrupt judges sought to incite the people against him. As part of his defense, he recited a litany of macro event-evidence, including Moses and the Red Sea, Moses and the brass serpent, the testimony of Abraham, the testimonies of Zenos, Zenock, Ezias, Isaiah, and Jeremiah, the destruction of Jerusalem, and the testimonies of father Lehi and his son Nephi (Helaman 8:11, 14, 18–23).

After the bold enumeration of these events he stated for emphasis, "And now, seeing ye know these things and cannot deny them except ye shall lie, therefore in this ye have sinned, for ye have rejected all these things, *notwithstanding so many evidences which ye have received*; yea, even ye have received all things, both things in heaven, and all things which are in the earth, as a witness that they are true" (Helaman 8:24; emphasis added).

It is remarkable to note that Nephi's use of the word "evidences" and his understanding of macroevents as evidence of God's hand corresponds completely with the manner in which we have been employing the term.

In our current latter-day setting, we often use event evidence in our exhortations for increased faith and testimony. We speak of the Prophet's first vision, the angel Moroni, the coming forth of the Book of Mormon, the visit of John the Baptist and Peter, James, and John, the dedication of the Kirtland Temple, Zion's Camp, the incomparable pioneer trek west, the seagulls and the crickets, and the "unbelievable" growth of the church and temples that begin to dot the land. These events and many more are referenced every Sunday as evidence upon which we encourage Latter-day Saints to build their faith.

Past events, together with the scriptures and the heavens

47

and earth, the handiwork of God, all fit into the category of macroevidence. Individually, these are significant evidences; collectively, they provide a powerful body of touchable, feelable, investigatable evidence of the reality of God and his desire to bless his children.

Alma gave us a helpful summary of macroevidence (and mortal assurances) when he said to Korihor: "Will ye say, Show unto me a sign, when ye have the testimony of all these thy brethren, and also all the holy prophets? The scriptures are laid before thee, yea, and all things denote there is a God; yea, even the earth, and all things that are upon the face of it, yea, and its motion, yea, and also all the planets which move in their regular form do witness that there is a Supreme Creator" (Alma 30:41).

MICROEVIDENCE

What about microevidence? Microevidence is a convenient classification for all the personal and individual experiences that each of us has that serve as evidence of the hand of God. These are private, often sacred, experiences. Some can be shared; some ought not be. Individual promptings, answers to prayers, divine protection, and healings are examples of this kind of evidence.

Descriptions of these personal spiritual experiences abound in both ancient and modern prophetic writings, as well as in current Church literature. The *Ensign, Church News,* and other Church publications contain numerous descriptions of individual member experiences that fit into the category of microevidence. We recognize the link between evidence and faith by referring to these accounts as *faith-promoting* stories or experiences. It is important to recognize that these experiences are most often designed to bless individual lives, and are not intended for self-aggrandizement or personal currency. Indeed, when we use these special manifestations inappropriately, they will usually cease.

STORIES OF MICROEVIDENCE IN THE SCRIPTURES

Though the scriptures as a whole are macroevidence, in individual passages they can also be a good source of appropriately shared expressions of microevidence. Consider two found in the Book of Mormon.

In Alma 36, Alma the Younger speaks to his son Helaman and shares his personal experience of being visited by an angel. He uses the experience to provide to Helaman assurances of the existence of God and the divine mission of Jesus Christ in atoning for the sins of the world. After his description of this dramatic, soul-changing vision, Alma recites other personal evidence. He says, "And I have been supported under trials and troubles of every kind, yea, and in all manner of afflictions; yea, God has delivered me from prison, and from bonds, and from death; yea, and I do put my trust in him, and he will still deliver me" (Alma 36:27).

As a second example of shared microevidence, we can read the eloquent statement of personal struggles and resulting faith expressed by Nephi in what is sometimes called "Nephi's Psalm." (I will quote only excerpts, but the entire passage deserves a complete reading and re-reading.)

Nephi begins by describing feelings that we have all had. He says, "Notwithstanding the great goodness of the Lord, in showing me his great and marvelous works [in other words, Nephi is rehearsing the evidences he has seen], my heart exclaimeth: O wretched man that I am! Yea, my heart sorroweth because of my flesh; my soul grieveth because of mine iniquities. . . . And when I desire to rejoice, my heart groaneth because of my sins."

But then he exclaims, "Nevertheless, I know in whom I have trusted. My God hath been my support; he hath led me . . . ; and he hath preserved me. . . . He hath filled me with his love. . . . He hath confounded mine enemies. . . . He hath heard my cry . . . , and he hath given me knowledge by visions" (2 Nephi 4:17, 19–23).

After remembering God's continuing and powerful assistance to him, he cries out, "Awake, my soul! . . . Rejoice, O my heart. . . . Do not anger again. . . . Do not slacken my strength. . . . Rejoice, O my heart, and cry unto the Lord, and say: O Lord, I will praise thee forever; yea, my soul will rejoice in thee, my God, and the rock of my salvation" (2 Nephi 4:28–30). Then we read this phrase with such beautiful visual imagery: "O Lord, wilt thou encircle me around in the robe of thy righteousness!" (2 Nephi 4:33).

Nephi finishes with these final thoughts: "O Lord, I have trusted in thee, and I will trust in thee forever. I will not put my trust in the arm of flesh. . . . Yea, my God will give me, if I ask not amiss; therefore I will lift up my voice unto thee; yea, I will cry unto thee, my God, the rock of my righteousness. Behold, my voice shall forever ascend up unto thee, my rock and mine everlasting God." (2 Nephi 4:34–35).

Nephi had a wide range of spiritual experiences, and the emotional highs and lows that generally accompany them. Though he exclaimed at one point, "Oh wretched man that I am," his desire was to not allow his despair to slacken his resolve to continue keeping the commandments and praising the Lord for his goodness. We should be grateful to Nephi for his forthrightness and honesty in revealing the true feelings of his soul, and for his ability to communicate one of the most beautiful passages in all of scripture.

MICROEVIDENCES IN OUR OWN EXPERIENCE

We could cite many other examples of the blessing and insight that come from the spiritual experiences that have strengthened individuals and families. One purpose of family history is to preserve the personal evidence of one's own ancestors (and ourselves for our descendants), that the faith of future generations might be strengthened. We also love to hear and read stories about the prophets and apostles, both past and present, and the evidences they give us that build our faith.

I well remember such a personal experience in the recent history of my own family. With one of her pregnancies Margaret went into labor a month early. At about 3:00 A.M. on a beautiful June morning she gave birth to identical twin boys. After learning that she and the twins both seemed well, I was much relieved and went home for a few hours of sleep. At about 7:00 A.M. the phone rang. It was a call from the hospital explaining that the second twin was in serious trouble and I should come quickly. I called one of my counselors in the bishopric, who was also an administrator at the hospital, and asked if he could meet me there immediately. I knelt in prayer, pleading for help, and then rushed to the hospital, hoping to arrive in time to give the baby a priesthood blessing and, if necessary, a name.

We found the baby lying in an isolette, a specialized chamber for premature infants. He was blue and gasping for breath. To my dismay he was so small and hooked up to so many tubes and pieces of apparatus that we could find no way to place our hands on his head to administer a blessing. After some agonizing moments, we determined that there was a spot on his little chest about the size of a half dollar that perhaps we could touch. So, reaching under and through and around all the tubes and equipment, we were able to get the very tips of four enormous fingers on that one tiny spot on his chest. We blessed him that he would receive specialized medical attention, that his life would be spared, and that he and his brother would serve together as missionaries in the year 2000.

That day in our family we received some very personalized microevidence of the unseen power of God.

AN EXPANDED DEFINITION OF FAITH

After our analysis and illustrations we can now propose a completed, expanded definition of faith based on Hebrews 11:1. It is as follows:

Faith is having or accepting mortal assurances from priesthood leaders, family members, and

friends, and heavenly assurances from the
Holy Ghost, that Christ lived, atoned for our
sins, was resurrected, and promises eternal life.
Faith is accepting macroevidence of God in the
form of his creations, the scriptures, and
significant events, and microevidence in the
form of personal spiritual experiences.

As we have seen, this expanded definition of faith contains
four elements. They are (1) mortal assurances, (2) heavenly
assurances, (3) macroevidence, and (4) microevidence. Having
a well-developed definition of faith makes it possible to do several interesting and potentially useful things. First, we can
answer questions that are often asked about faith, such as, What
is faith? How can I know if I have it? Where does it come from?
Second, we can introduce the notion of a faith "diagnosis" and
use it to suggest useful "prescriptions."

QUESTIONS ABOUT FAITH

Some may be blessed to have faith and to act on it without
question or analysis. But many individuals at some time or other
will ask the question, What is faith? To them we can say that
faith (following the definition in Hebrews 11:1) is accepting
assurances and evidence that Jesus Christ lived, is the Son of
God, atoned for our sins, was resurrected, and promises eternal
life. We can explain that faith need not be mystical or undefinable. We can assert that those who have faith are not naive
nor have they been duped. Rather, they have been willing to

entertain the possibility that assurances offered and evidences cited have merit and warrant further consideration. After consideration has been given and judgment rendered as to the source and reliability of the evidence, they have recognized that believing is a wise and reasoned response.

When we understand assurances and evidences, we have insight into the origin of personal faith. When asked, "Where does faith come from?" we may respond that for some it is a gift. But for others it comes as Alma described from the process of planting a seed and learning about assurances and evidences. The hearing, reading, and feeling that are involved with any learning process are applicable to learning about faith. Our faith will be strengthened as we receive assurances, ponder evidence, and pray for insight and understanding of what we have heard or read.

A DIAGNOSIS OF FAITH

Some may say, "I think I have faith but I'm not sure. How can I tell?" This can be a very helpful question, because answering it requires a diagnosis and implies the possibility of a subsequent prescription.

Consider the possibility of using our definition of faith as a basis for a faith "diagnosis." In the same way that a mechanic might diagnose car problems or a physician diagnose medical problems, we may be able to develop a diagnosis for anemic faith. Instead of four basic nutrition groups, we could recommend four basic spiritual food groups. We could propose that a healthy faith would include a balanced "diet" of each of the four kinds of assurances and evidences. And in the same way that poor health could be diagnosed as a lack of protein or vegetables in a diet, so weak faith could be diagnosed as a lack of one or another kind of assurance or evidence. Questions could be developed with the purpose of identifying the particular deficiency. With loving kindness, a priesthood leader or friend might prescribe a diet rich in assurances from general conference or macroevidence from the scriptures as the way to build a healthy, vigorous faith.

This faith diagnosis could also be helpful in the home. We believe that parents have the responsibility to be proactive in helping their children develop faith. A mother and a father might do well to discuss whether or not they are providing their children with a healthy "serving" from each of the four groups. For example, it is possible for parents to teach from the scriptures and encourage their reading without including the essential element of the parents' own verbalized and frequently borne personal witnesses. In a similar vein, it is extremely useful for children not just to read about spiritual experiences but to hear of the personal evidence that parents have concerning protective promptings, the payment of tithing, and the healing power of the priesthood.

In another vein, public school curriculum in the United States has become so secularized that some young people may be reluctant to acknowledge the biblical view of creation. It is incumbent upon parents to provide supplementary reading and discussion opportunities that children might develop appreciation of the creation of the universe as evidence of God's handiwork. Firsthand encounters with the beauties of nature, organized and orchestrated by thoughtful and observant adults, have been the foundation of faith for a host of God's believing children.

The diagnosis and prescription for building vigorous faith can also play a vital role in missionary work. Consider the following prescription for investigators:

Rx for Investigator Faith

1. Establish the beginnings of faith with large doses of mortal assurances. These may come from:

    a. Missionaries, as they bear testimony on the doorstep, in discussions, and so forth.

    b. Relatives (Of course, the reason relatives provide successful referrals is that they are believable sources of mortal assurances.)

    c. Friends (Another believable source.)

2. Continue with nourishment of macroevidence from the scriptures, reading from the Bible and Book of Mormon.

3. Add microevidence as you help them recognize answered prayers, promptings, protections, and so forth.

4. Stir together the above ingredients to set the stage for receiving heavenly assurances from the Holy Ghost, as indicated in Moroni's promise:

"And when ye shall receive these things, I would exhort you that ye would ask God, the Eternal Father, in the name of Christ, if these things are not true; and if ye shall ask with a sincere heart, with real intent, having faith in Christ, he will manifest the truth of it unto you, by the power of the Holy Ghost" (Moroni 10:4).

A prescription for reactivating or rekindling the faith of current members would contain the same ingredients, but might include words such as *recall, remind, rehearse,* and *review,* for example, (1) *recalling* mortal assurances that have been given them, (2) *reminding* them of feelings they've had as they received heavenly assurances, (3) *rehearsing* the macroevidence from the scriptures, and (4) *reviewing* their own personal religious experiences. These reminding experiences could be supplemented with new and fresh ingredients until the result is renewed, revitalized, and reinvigorated faith.

3

$\mathcal{A}$ $\mathcal{G}raphic$ $\mathcal{V}iew$
OF FAITH

"I sat in my room pondering over the scriptures."

D&C 138:1

S ome people learn better verbally, some visually. To help broaden our understanding of faith, in this chapter we will look at a series of elementary graphs designed to visually stimulate individual insights and personal observations about the process of developing faith. We will also consider the question of whether one of the four elements of faith is more important than another and whether or not it is possible (or desirable) to measure the difference in impact or influence of each of these elements. Most of the ideas in this chapter can be understood by looking at the pictures. But if this kind of presentation is intimidating to you (not a few of us suffer math anxiety!), feel free to move past it to the next chapter.

It is common in the social sciences to "model" a process or relationship in order to investigate its properties and understand the underlying relationship. A model is generally built to present an abstract idea or concept in simple and easily understood terms.

The first step in modeling is to express a relationship in words, which is what we have done in the preceding chapters on faith. The next step is to associate words with symbols. Think of symbols as word-saving communication devices. For example, in high school algebra, we learn that "X" and "Y" are symbols often used to stand for words. If Y is the symbol for income and X is the symbol for education, then Y has some relationship to or depends on X.

MODELING THE GROWTH OF FAITH

We are now in a position to model the working definition of faith developed in chapters 1 and 2. In those chapters we suggested that faith is related to mortal assurances, heavenly assurances, macroevidence, and microevidence. We can further investigate the nature of these relationships through the technique of modeling, using a series of graphs. Any proposed relationship can be visually depicted by plotting the relationship on a graph with an X and Y axis. This graphing or modeling is nothing more than a form of pondering, where we think about and think through important eternal truths.

Consider, for example, figure 2. Figure 2 proposes one kind of relationship between faith and mortal assurances. In this relationship, faith grows slowly and gradually with the addition of each new mortal assurance. Contrast that with the relationship shown in figure 3. In figure 3 faith is again shown as growing with mortal assurances, but the growth is much more rapid.

Figures 2 and 3 both suggest that faith increases proportionately with increases in mortal assurances. Figure 2, however, proposes that it would require very many assurances to have much impact on faith, whereas figure 3 implies each additional assurance has a major impact on faith.

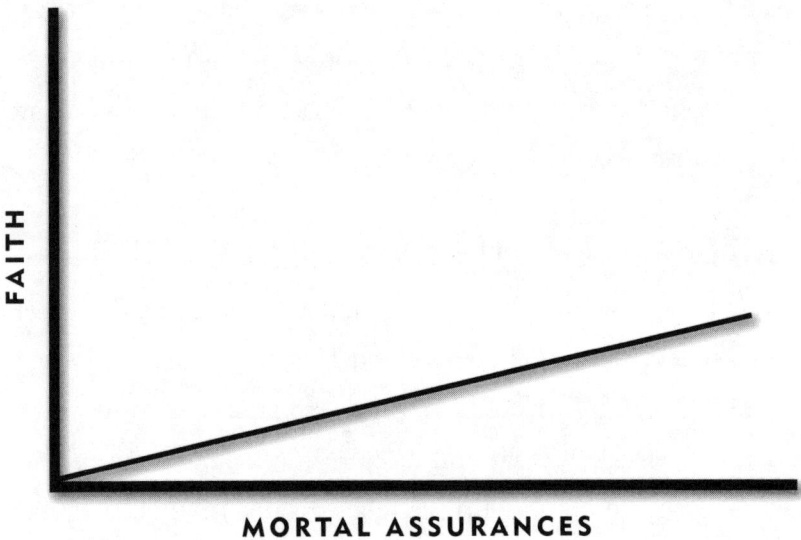

MORTAL ASSURANCES

Figure 2

Which is the case in real life? Perhaps both models are correct, depending on the circumstances. For instance, figure 2 might depict the growth of a person's faith if the mortal assurances received do not make much of an impression; this might be due to the nature of the individual(s) providing the assurance, the setting, or the receptivity of the listener. On the other hand, with figure 3 one or more of these elements may combine

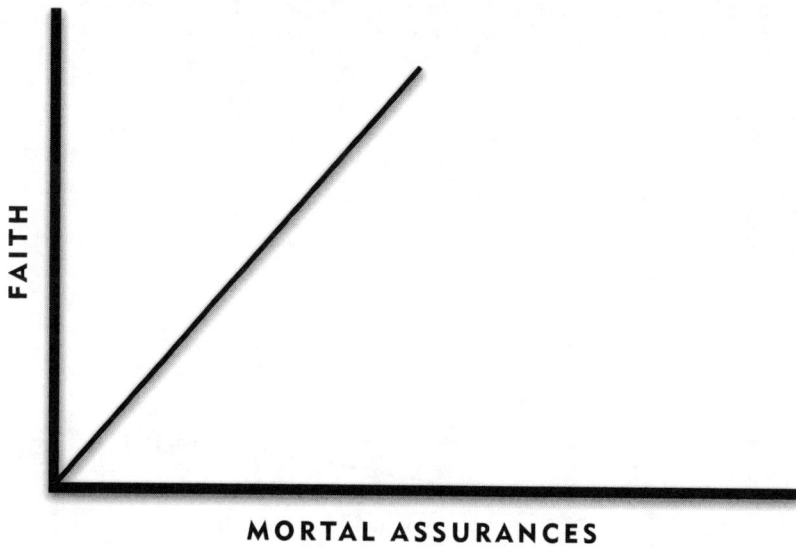

MORTAL ASSURANCES

Figure 3

to greatly increase the person's faith. The person might have greater regard for the individual providing the assurance, or the setting might be more conducive for the person to receive the assurance, or the person's circumstances in life might make him or her more receptive—or all of the above.

"Doubting" Thomas, the apostle who was so called because of his unwillingness to believe the mortal assurance of the other apostles, is a biblical example of figure 2, where faith is affected little by mortal assurances. After personally appearing to Thomas to dispel his doubt, the Savior said, "Thomas, because thou hast seen me, thou hast believed: blessed are they that have not seen, and yet have believed" (John 20:29). Those who believe without seeing, who readily accept personal witnesses, testimonies, and assurances, are blessed with the growth of faith depicted in figure 3.

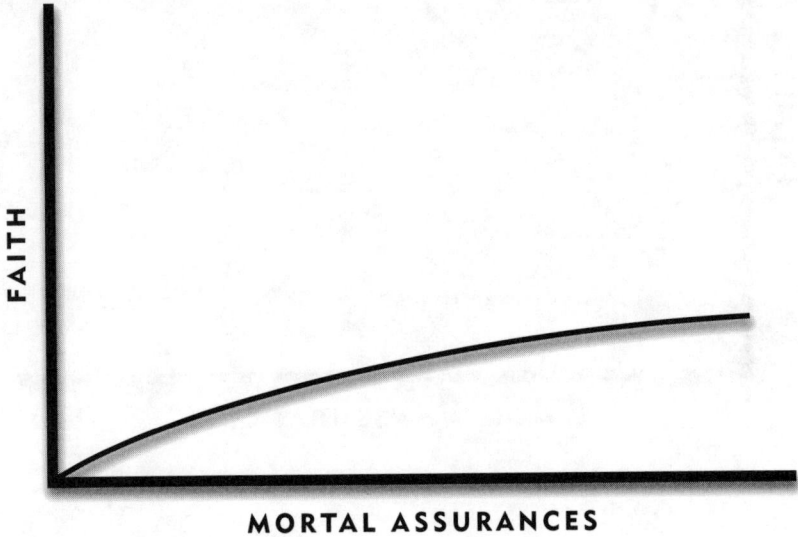

MORTAL ASSURANCES

Figure 4

Figure 4 shows us another way in which faith may grow.

In this case, faith increases quickly with initial mortal assurances, but begins to level off as each additional assurance adds to faith. Each additional assurance does increase faith, but by a diminishing amount each time.

Please understand that this chapter is not intended to describe exactly how a given individual's faith grows. Instead, we seek to stimulate individual insights and personal observations about one's own faith development process. As you consider your own experience with faith and mortal assurances, would you say that it most resembles figure 2, 3, or 4? Would you graphically plot your faith as a gradual upward slope, a more rapid upward slope, or a gradual curve that levels off? If your faith based on mortal assurances grows slowly, what would help it to grow more quickly? Perhaps the answer is that you need to seek mortal assurances from sources you regard more highly, or you may need to be more open to what you receive. Or perhaps the answer can be found by seeking a different kind of assurance.

FAITH AND HEAVENLY ASSURANCES

Let's now consider the relationship between faith and heavenly assurances. It may be argued that heavenly assurances would have a very significant impact on faith. A possible relationship may look like the one proposed in figure 5.

In figure 5 the slope of the line is upward, or positive, meaning that faith is always increasing with any additional assurance.

HEAVENLY ASSURANCES

Figure 5

But unlike in previous figures, in figure 5 we posit that the slope of the line does not level off, but rather increases in steepness, meaning that additional heavenly assurances *accelerate* the growth in faith. We all know from experience that a witness of the Holy Ghost, or other legitimate spiritual manifestations, can have a dramatic impact on faith. In fact, in some cases the growth in faith may be as dramatic as that shown in figure 6.

HEAVENLY ASSURANCES

Figure 6

The relationship between faith and heavenly assurances depicted in figure 6 may describe Saul's experience, as recounted in Acts 9. On his way to Damascus to continue his "threaten-ings and slaughter against the disciples of the Lord" (Acts 9:1), Saul had a vision in which the Lord appeared to him. Concerning Saul the Lord later said to Ananias, "He is a chosen vessel unto me, to bear my name before the Gentiles, and kings, and the children of Israel" (Acts 9:15). Ananias subsequently explained to Saul, "The Lord, even Jesus, that appeared unto thee in the way . . . hath sent me, that thou mightest receive thy sight, and be filled with the Holy Ghost" (Acts 9:17). "And *straightway* [Saul] preached Christ in the synagogues, that he is the Son of God" (Acts 9:20; emphasis added).

Saul's acquisition of faith in Christ was not a gradual or continuous process. Rather it came in a singular, sudden, and momentous event in which Saul received a heavenly assurance from the Lord himself. That assurance was reinforced as Saul was filled with the Holy Ghost. Figure 6 models this dramatic acquisition of faith as a vertical, straight line. (Certainly as Saul, now Paul, subsequently grew in his faith in particular principles, he may have done so following a different model.)

How has your own faith grown when you have experienced heavenly assurances? I would suspect that that growth has been significant—perhaps sometimes like figure 5, or even sometimes like figure 6. Of course, as most members of the Church can testify, one does not need an extraordinary heavenly manifestation to have accelerated faith. The power of the Holy Ghost in one's everyday life is real and quite sufficient to have a dramatic impact on faith.

Remember that having faith is receiving or accepting both mortal and heavenly assurances of the reality of Christ, the resurrection, and eternal life. These graphs suggest that faith can increase with additional assurances of each kind, but it can be dramatically strengthened by heavenly assurances.

FAITH, MACROEVIDENCES, AND MICROEVIDENCES

As we discussed in chapter 2, faith is also a function of macroevidence and microevidence. We have defined macroevidence as large or global evidence. This would include both the heavens and the earth as the handiwork of God; the scriptures, which describe his dealings with his children on earth; and significant events where his power has been manifest. Microevidence consists of those personal evidences that are individual in nature. It could include answers to prayer, blessings from priesthood administrations, and other individual spiritual experiences.

Figures 7 and 8 suggest possible relationships between the growth of faith and macroevidence and microevidence.

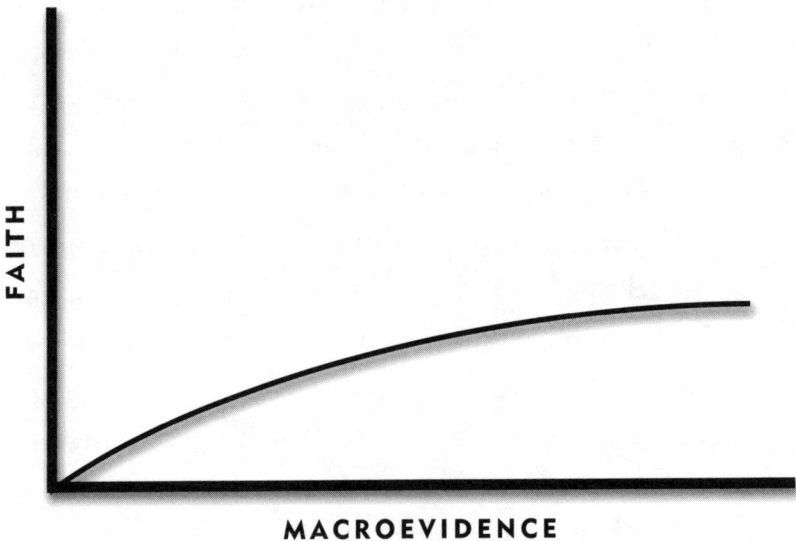

MACROEVIDENCE

Figure 7

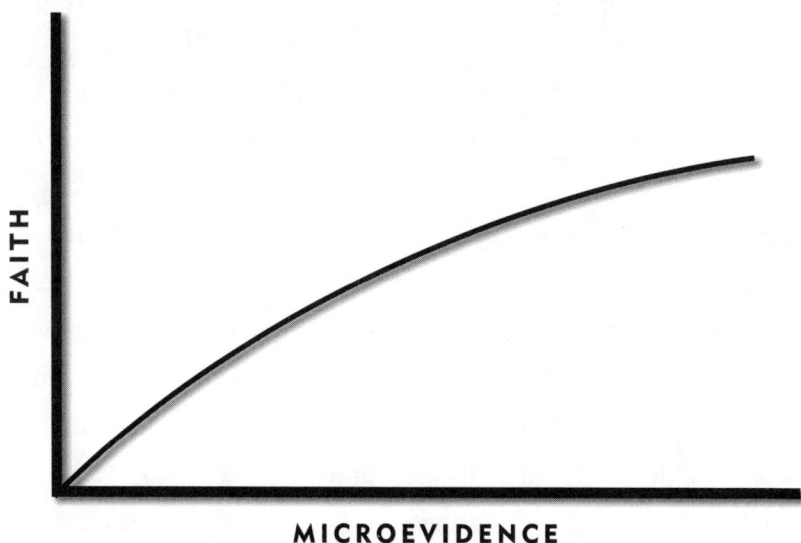

Figure 8

Note that in both cases it is proposed that faith increases with additional evidence of either kind. Both cases also assume that additional evidence has less and less impact or has decreasing marginal value to the building of faith. Perhaps your own experience is different, but it seems that the faith of most people grows to a particular level (whether quickly or slowly) and then seems to plateau. In pondering about your own growth of faith, it would be well to ask if this has been your experience—and if faith necessarily has an upward limit, or if it could continue to grow indefinitely.

The difference between figures 7 and 8 is that one has a steeper slope than the other. This suggests the possibility that individual experiences have a greater impact on faith than more global but less personal experiences. But this is certainly a proposition that is open to discussion—and specific counter examples can be generated. For instance, as the title page to the Book of Mormon clearly states, it is intended that the book (which we have labeled as macroevidence), have a major impact on faith in Christ. Therefore, one might argue that the curves proposed in figures 7 and 8 should look more the same—or be reversed. On the other hand, the real power of the Book of Mormon comes as the Holy Ghost testifies of its truthfulness (an experience we have labeled as microevidence or heavenly assurance). Perhaps once again we see that microevidences and macroevidences, and mortal assurances and heavenly assurances, are inextricably intertwined, and that it is difficult to receive one in a faith-promoting manner without receiving the other.

In any case, it is important to note that our pondering is not being done in a modern attempt to imitate the Pharisees. The process of modeling and questioning is meant to give us understanding and insight into our own faith and its development. It is a vehicle for discussion and investigation of an intangible construct.

It is equally important to realize that we are not suggesting faith can be translated into mathematics. Neither are we making the argument that by associating faith with graphs and symbols we are somehow giving scientific proof to a deeply religious and spiritual concept. Rather, as was suggested at the outset, we are employing a visual technique to broaden our understanding and assist in the learning process.

ADVANCED PONDERING ON THE PROCESS OF FAITH

As we continue to seek insight into the growth of faith—and how it relates to our own experiences—let's consider an interesting final extension of our analysis.* To focus on the *process* of developing faith, and to underscore the interrelationship of the varying sources of faith, let's briefly combine our four categories of assurances and evidences under two headings: mortal evidences and assurances and heavenly evidences and assurances. We would move much of macroevidence to the "mortal" heading, and much of microevidence (which includes individual spiritual experiences) to the "heavenly" heading. We would then propose that these two categories have the familiar graphic shapes shown in figures 9 and 10.

We noted earlier that mortal or earthly experience (assurances) seems to provide diminishing returns over time, placing limits or bounds on our faith. In other words, *if we entertain only the witness of other persons and the physical evidence available for us to see and touch, our faith cannot grow beyond a certain level.* Our faith is constrained, limited, and bounded by the nature of the assurances and evidences we are willing or able to consider. Therefore, if we do not make efforts to also acquire heavenly evidences and assurances, a fullness of faith cannot be reached.

If heavenly evidences and assurances are sought and received, however, and if they increase or accelerate as we have

---

*Proposed in discussions with Stan Fawcett, a faculty colleague at Brigham Young University.

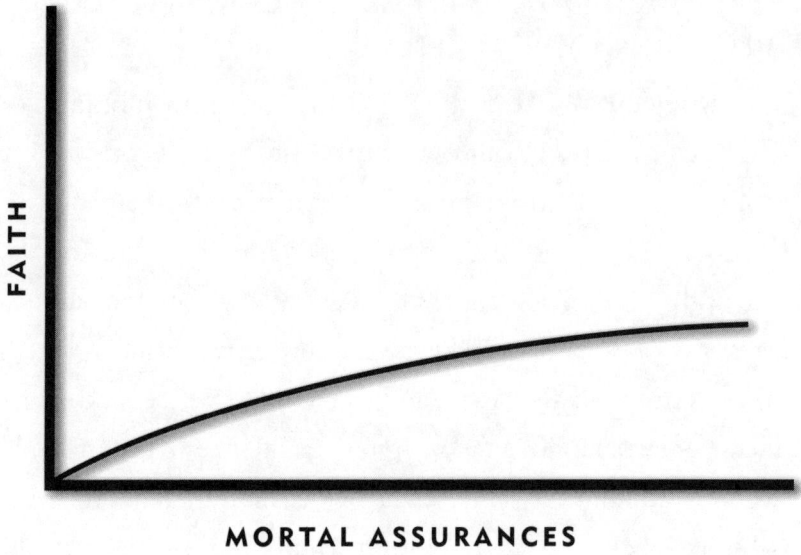

MORTAL ASSURANCES

Figure 9

HEAVENLY ASSURANCES

Figure 10

suggested they might, then the path of faith or the process by which it is developed may be depicted as shown in figure 11.

Our supposition with figure 11 is that the acceptance of mortal assurances and macroevidence (or external evidence) is a *beginning* of the process. These evidences are generally available to each individual on earth, to a greater or lesser degree. However, faith has an upward limit inherent in the idea that there are decreasing marginal returns to certain kinds of evidence.

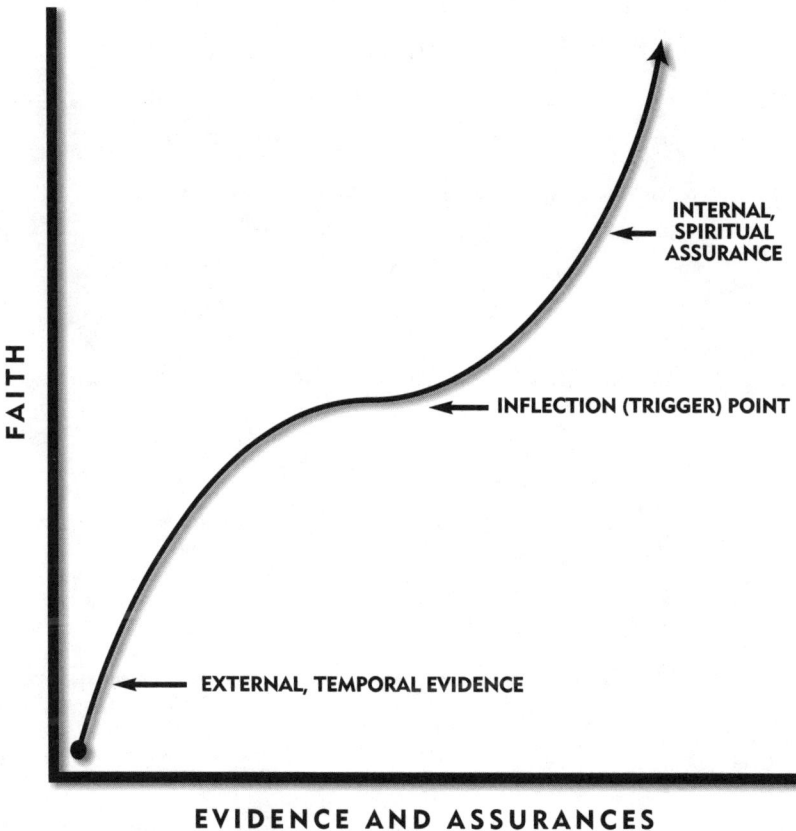

INTERNAL, SPIRITUAL ASSURANCE

INFLECTION (TRIGGER) POINT

EXTERNAL, TEMPORAL EVIDENCE

FAITH

EVIDENCE AND ASSURANCES

Figure 11

How do we pass the point where our faith has begun to level off (called the "inflection point") and move on to experience the upward growth in faith? Or how do we move beyond mortal assurances and on to heavenly assurances of the things hoped for? The keys are diligence and faithfulness in actively seeking after God. Recall that in chapter 1, while discussing how faith may begin with the receipt of personal assurances, we used the diagram reproduced here as figure 12.

In figure 12, we suggested that the dot in the lower left-hand corner could represent the seed of faith spoken of by Alma. There we examined how the seed of faith grows through mortal and heavenly assurances. Now, with our combined categories, we can relabel this diagram to look at mortal evidences and assurances and heavenly evidences and assurances. Figures 11 and 12 can then be combined to create the diagram in figure 13.

The upward curving line in figure 13 traces the path of faith. It starts as a seed, represented by the small dot in the box

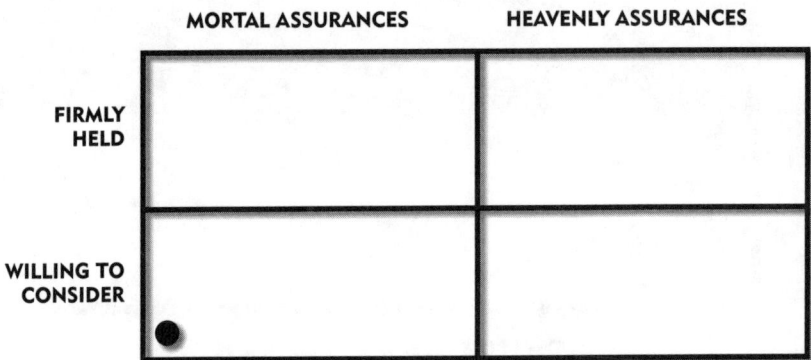

Figure 12

MORTAL ASSURANCES AND EVIDENCES   **HEAVENLY ASSURANCES AND EVIDENCES**

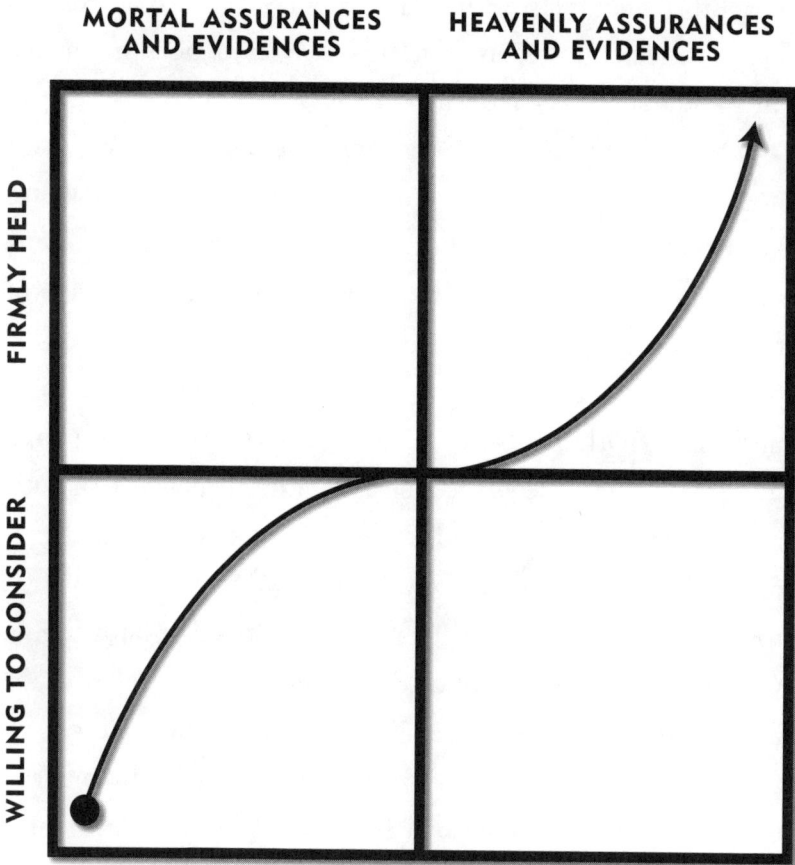

Figure 13

labeled Willing to Consider/Mortal Assurances and Evidences. Faith grows as more mortal assurances are received and as macroevidence is considered and accepted. But as we observed earlier, if we entertain only the witness of other people and the physical evidence available for us to see and touch, our faith cannot grow beyond certain limited bounds. As we see in figure 13, if we desire our faith to continue to grow, we must progress beyond the boundary of mortal evidences and assurances and begin to seek and receive the heavenly evidences and assurances that are associated with unbounded faith.

At the beginning of these chapters on faith I put forth two notions. The first was that faith need not be an ethereal and hazily defined concept, but rather one for which a clear definition can be established. The second is that the acquisition of faith may be thought of as a process with beginning steps, a probable path, and the hoped-for outcome of complete and unshakable faith in Christ. In the pages that followed, we have indeed been able to come to a clear definition of faith, that faith is accepting assurances and evidences of Christ's atonement, resurrection, and promise of eternal life. We have also been able to propose a process for developing faith. It is that faith begins with personal assurances offered by parents, friends, relatives, or missionaries. These personal assurances act as the seed spoken of by Alma. To personal assurances we can add the macro-evidences that essentially come from three places: the earth and heavens as God's handiwork, the scriptures, and significant events.

The limiting element of mortal evidences and assurances is overcome as our effort to actively seek the Lord leads to individual spiritual experiences and the heavenly assurances available from the Holy Ghost. Jacob acknowledged the process by describing it this way: "Wherefore, we search the prophets [receive personal assurances], and we have many revelations [individual spiritual experiences] and the spirit of prophecy [heavenly assurance from the Holy Ghost]; and having all these witnesses [both mortal and heavenly assurances and evidences] we obtain a hope, and our faith becometh unshaken" (Jacob 4:6). What a wonderful blessing to have unshaken faith in Christ. No greater blessing could come to any of God's children than to know his Son as Savior and Redeemer.

4

$\mathcal{J}$ustification

"Therefore being justified by faith, we have peace with God through our Lord Jesus Christ."

ROMANS 5:1

The assertion that faith is a wonderful blessing is usually accepted without question, even by unbelievers. We somehow intuitively recognize that we are better off because we believe in something or someone beyond ourselves. Like the boy with the helium-filled balloons, most of us feel a lifting, buoying force in our lives, and our gaze is extended upward toward heaven. But there is more to faith than good feelings and improved mental posture—much more! We have earlier read the scripture, "Therefore being *justified by faith*, we have peace with God through our Lord Jesus Christ: By whom also we have access by faith into this *grace* wherein we stand, and rejoice in hope of the glory of God" (Romans 5:1–2; emphasis added). To learn about the "much more" that faith represents, we must investigate what it means to be *justified by faith*, that we might have "peace with God through our Lord Jesus Christ." In the process we will also want to understand what Paul means by the concept of having "access by faith into . . . grace."

The principle of justification is critical to our understanding of the plan of redemption and the atoning sacrifice of the Savior. It is a concept not often spoken about, but nevertheless it is one of substantial significance. Understanding justification is important because it is a key element in the process by which the atoning blood of the Savior is applied in our lives. Understanding this process makes abundantly clear the role of faith in the eternal scheme of things.

The dictionary defines *justification* as "the act of justifying" or "the condition of being justified." It further defines *justify* as (1) to demonstrate or prove to be just, right, or valid; (2) to show to be well-founded or warranted; (3) to declare free of blame.

Since these definitions are rather abstract, some illustrations would surely be helpful. If you do any word processing, you may recognize the word *justified* in the context of right or left justified margins. This means that the typed words all fit exactly against the right margin or left margin. When the words are all justified, we can instantly see that the margins are exact and without error.

Similarly, we may question in our writing whether each word is spelled correctly. We know if we hand our English teacher a paper that contains misspelled words, we will be penalized for not being exact. We can tackle the spelling challenge in several ways. We could look at each word and declare, "Well, that looks right to me." This is an excellent example of self-justification or self-validation. If we are more exacting or not so sure of ourselves, we could examine a dictionary and let Noah Webster serve the validating or warranting function vis à vis our spelling exactness. We also have the option of running the spell-checking routine on our word processor, which will let the computer "justify" our work.

In finance and accounting the numbers or data are validated, or justified, by a third party called an auditor. With taxes, the Internal Revenue Service requires taxpayers to report their income and their federal tax liability according to a complicated set of rules. These tax returns are examined periodically by an auditor, whose job it is to determine whether or not the rules were followed with exactness. If they were not followed correctly or exactly, the taxpayer is not "justified" and may be subject to penalties.

In fact, in each of these three illustrations there are penalties for inexactness. In the case of left or right justification of the margins of our paper, the penalty is not too severe. The paper may look a little sloppy or may have to be realigned to satisfy a English teacher or thesis adviser. Similarly, we can correct misspelled words, or we may decide to accept the five-point penalty and go on our way. Failing an IRS audit may be more serious and can result in financial or even legal penalties. This is true even if the return was prepared in good faith and the taxpayer believed all the rules were being followed.

THE CHALLENGE OF EXACTNESS

Our experience with exactness teaches us that there are "soft" rules and "hard" rules, varying "allowances," and varying "penalties" attached for inexactness. In fact, part of living a happy and successful life is to sort out all the rules, allowances, and penalties that apply to our differing circumstances. This is certainly true for young people, who face what they may perceive to be an unnecessary number of often bewildering parental, school, and societal rules. Some of these rules may or may not be followed with exactness. For example, "Son, tonight's a school night—be in by 10:30" provides a wonderful opportunity to experience the concept of fuzzy logic. Or how about, "We'll be gone for the weekend; don't put too many miles on the car"?

Once when our boys were little, Margaret left them with a babysitter to go out to lunch with some former college roommates. She invited the friends home afterward to visit. As they walked in the door Margaret thought she smelled smoke, and a few moments later she saw the boys hurrying downstairs to the basement, each carrying glasses of water. Being an experienced mother of boys, she excused herself and followed them quickly to the basement. It seemed, while the babysitter was busy with the twins, the other boys had decided to go to the basement and build a fort. They pulled out the hide-a-bed from the couch, draped blankets over the edges of the bed to make walls, and crawled in under the mattress to their fort. Their fort was dark but, ever resourceful, they lit a nice big candle to provide a cheery glow. After a minute or two the candle had caught the ceiling of their fort—which was the bottom of the mattress—on fire. Undaunted, they went to the nearby fireplace and returned with the big fireplace bellows, which they felt sure they could use to blow out the fire. By and by, they realized there seemed to be a flaw in the "blow it out" theory.

So they went to Plan B, which was the "drown it out" concept. When Margaret entered on the scene they were trying to figure out how to crawl into the fort and splash the water up out of the glasses and onto the underside of the mattress. Margaret did the smart thing: she grabbed the mattress off the hide-a-bed, tossed it through the patio door into the backyard—and began to contemplate the color she would like for her new couch. Later, Margaret was discussing the incident with the sitter's mother. The mother observed that the daughter felt bad about what had happened and said it would have been helpful to her daughter to have had more exact household rules to follow. For a long while after that we communicated clearly to each babysitter our rule number one: "Don't let the boys burn down the house!"

On a more serious and tender note, I know a person who is coming to the end of a life extremely well lived. This man has a wonderful posterity, including accomplished children and consistently faithful grandchildren. He is loved and revered in his community and known for his wisdom, wit, and generosity. He has served his Heavenly Father diligently all his life and is a model of Christianity in thought and action.

And yet in his great and tender heart there is a sadness and angst. He worries about a younger brother—a brother who has struggled and for whom life has not been sweet. For this struggling brother my friend has provided love, tender counsel, food, appliances, clothes, and mortgage payments; he has been there in every way possible to lift and succor. To our collective dismay the brother believes that he has been mistreated by my friend, and my friend is left to weep and wonder if he has done all that he could or should do. We who have observed have tried diligently to convince him that he has more than met any reasonable test of Christian exactness. He has been somewhat but not totally consoled by our urgings.

In these two situations we have examples of the dilemmas we face as we try to grapple with the notion of exactness in our lives. Sometimes, as in the case of the babysitter, we may not perceive the rules to be clear. Other times we may, like my friend, agonize over whether or not we have done all that we could to conform our lives to gospel principles. Our reasoned response to these dilemmas is to feel that if we do our best, everything will turn out all right. To some extent that may be true, but it is very important that we understand how it is that things *can* turn out all right and how Heavenly Father views the issues of exactness and justification.

GOD'S VIEW OF EXACTNESS

In the gospel context, of course, the issue is not exactness in margins, spelling rules, or IRS guidelines but in keeping God's laws. Justification involves a validation or warranty of whether or not God's laws were kept with exactness. Heavenly Father's notion of exactness is quite clear. In the book of Alma we read, "Neither can filthiness or anything which is unclean be received into the kingdom of God" (Alma 7:21). In a later chapter Alma further observes, "For the Lord cannot look upon sin with the least degree of allowance" (Alma 45:16). Using almost the same words, the Lord himself explained to the Prophet Joseph Smith, "For I the Lord cannot look upon sin with the least degree of allowance" (D&C 1:31).

The phrase "least degree of allowance" is very descriptive. It makes it clear that when it comes to the Lord's requirement, there is no wiggle room with regard to anything that is unclean, filthy, or sinful. In other words the Lord's standard is perfect exactness. Every "letter" has to line up perfectly in the "margin," all "words" must be "spelled" exactly, and every regulation must be followed to the letter of the law. That may seem like an impossible standard. We are used to operating with considerably more fuzziness in our borders and guidelines. We may react by considering such an exacting standard to be harsh or unloving. But this is not the case.

It would be a great mistake to look upon God as "hard line" or too demanding. God just does things right—perfectly and exactly right. That is what we should expect if we believe in a God who is perfect in every dimension and aspect of his character. But in the face of such exactness it is understandable for us to throw our hands in the air and exclaim, "This is impossible! Nobody's perfect! Give me a break, for heaven's sake!"

THE COMPLIANCE OFFICER

And indeed, heaven does give us a break. Let me explain it first in secular terms. Consider the example of a defense contractor, a company that manufactures ships, airplanes, tanks, or other items for the United States Department of Defense. When a defense contractor is awarded a federal contract, the agreement clearly indicates that the specifications of the contract must be followed or the contractor will suffer certain penalties. The contractor is aware of both the rigor of the specifications and the associated penalties and agrees to them as a condition of receiving the contract.

Once the contractor is awarded the contract, he doesn't complain that it is unfair to be held to certain standards of performance. In fact, the contractor himself employs a "compliance officer" to help ensure that all contractual standards are being met. It is the responsibility of the compliance officer to report any deviations or inexactness to the contractor so that they may be corrected *before* the errors come to the attention of the government inspectors. In this manner the contractor assures himself that he can deliver a product that meets the exact specifications of the contract and that there will be no penalties imposed.

In a similar manner, most business firms employ an internal auditor who has the responsibility of identifying any transactions, practices, or accounting approaches that do not comply with accepted accounting standards. Deviations from standards are reported to company officials so that appropriate corrective action can be taken *before* outside auditors bring the problems to the attention of directors and shareholders.

A HEAVENLY "COMPLIANCE OFFICER"

Now consider our Heavenly Father's approach to "giving us a break" in the matter of exactness and justification. We read in

Moses 6:60: "For by the water ye keep the commandment; by the Spirit ye are justified, and by the blood ye are sanctified." This verse contains three important concepts and provides a critical insight into the principle of justification.

The first concept is that of baptism. The phrase "For by the water ye keep the commandment" points out that we are commanded to observe the *ordinance* of baptism by water if we are to enter into the kingdom of God. By being baptized we keep a commandment.

Justification, though, is not a commandment but a *principle* and a *process*. We learn that "by the Spirit ye are justified." In other words, the process of determining exactness in keeping the law is overseen by the Spirit. Or, to put it in somewhat secular but perhaps better understood terms, in God's economy the "compliance officer" is the Holy Ghost. The Holy Ghost keeps track of how well we comply with the laws of God. He is the internal auditor charged with determining how closely we follow correct principles.

The importance of the justification process cannot be overstated. It is the very process by which it is determined whether or not we merit the cleansing that comes from the atoning blood of the Savior. His sacrifice for sin will not be available to those who do not warrant it. We must meet certain conditions through obedience and repentance, and the Holy Ghost must warrant that this process is complete before we merit the sanctifying blessings of the atonement.

In other words, only after our compliance has been warranted *by the Spirit* will we be *sanctified by the blood*. That is why it is an extraordinary and merciful blessing, a heavenly "break," if you will, to have our own compliance officer or internal auditor. If our behavior is incompatible with God's laws we should hope and pray to be alerted to that fact. Any prompting, smallest hint, or subtlest indication from the Holy Ghost that we are "out of compliance" should be received with gratitude. Why? Because then we can take steps to avoid the penalties that will most certainly accompany our lack of compliance or exactness.

God leaves no doubt that penalties must be exacted if we fail to meet the requirements of the law. We read in Alma 42:22: "But there is a law given, and a punishment affixed, and a repentance granted; which repentance, mercy claimeth; otherwise, justice claimeth the creature and executeth the law, and the law inflicteth the punishment; if not so, the works of justice would be destroyed, and God would cease to be God."

The very important point here is that if we allow ourselves to be alerted by our personal compliance officer, the Holy Ghost, we can actuate a mechanism that provides a reprieve from the certain punishment. The mechanism, of course, is repentance, and the reprieve is God's forgiveness. The just-cited verse in Alma makes it clear: "There is a law given, and a punishment affixed, *and a repentance granted*" (emphasis added). God's laws do come with punishments affixed, but they also come with the possibility of a repentance granted.

How critical to our ultimate success is the phrase *a repentance granted!* If laws were given and punishments affixed with no possibility of repentance, we would be in a terrible fix. We would have to do everything exactly right the first time, and our punishments for inexactness would pile up rapidly. Instead of perceiving the Holy Ghost as our friend, we would recognize him as being there only to chronicle our every mistake. His job would be to make sure that justice was fully executed and that we received every punishment we deserved.

I suspect that under these circumstances we may *not* have voted in the premortal existence to support the plan of redemption presented by God. We would have found the plan to be perfectly just but would have recognized our inability to keep the laws with such exactness. Our fear of the "punishments affixed" with no possibility of relief may have made us very reluctant to embark on a mortal journey. Under those conditions, the learning process so necessary for growth likely would have appeared far too risky.

But, of course, God in his wisdom understood our fears and our weakness and affixed to the laws not only a punishment but also a possible repentance. Furthermore, he made it possible for us to know (if we desire it) when we are out of compliance with the law and need to repent to avoid the punishment.

COMPLIANCE PROBLEMS

There are at least three frequently encountered problems in the realm of secular compliance that have interesting gospel parallels. An individual moving towards compliance might ask:

1. What should I do about the past? I couldn't comply because I didn't know the rules, so I wish to be "held harmless" for past infractions.

2. Can we negotiate some interim period where the rules will be less rigorously enforced while I work toward compliance?

3. What about a "grandfather clause" that lets me operate under the *old* rules while new entities operate under the new rules?

What about the past? In the gospel there is a wonderful mechanism for dealing with past infractions and "holding harmless" the individual who sincerely did not know the law. This mechanism is "baptism by immersion for the remission of sins" (Articles of Faith 1:4). The effect of baptism (coupled with sincere repentance) is to wipe the old slate clean and provide a new starting point for keeping track of future compliance. In essence, we are told that we will not be punished for infractions that occurred prior to our knowledge of the laws.

However, there is a *quid pro quo*—something required for that which is given. In return for being held harmless for all past mistakes, we are expected to repent of those past mistakes—and try to be in full compliance in the future. As an added blessing, however, we are given a compliance officer to monitor and assist us. (Thus, the "compliance officer," the Holy Ghost, represents the Lord but also works to bless us in our efforts.) The responsibility of having to comply may at times seem like an unwanted burden. With some reflection, however, though some of us feel that "ignorance is bliss," we should prefer the power and progress that come with knowledge and responsibility.

What about an interim period of grace? The notion of an interim or transition period between noncompliance and full compliance is an interesting concept. It must stem from the realization that an organization or individual will require time to institute the processes and procedures necessary to comply with any new set of rules. The idea is that a lesser standard should be imposed while the organization is "learning." This is an appealing concept because it provides a positive incentive to make the changes necessary to comply. Our experience tells us that learning new behavior or changing old habits will not be instantaneous. A voice for negative incentives would say, "We want you to begin changing, and you'll be punished fully for every mistake you make while you're learning new behavior." The voice for positive incentives says, "We want you to change, and we'll overlook any mistakes you make during some reasonable interim period as long as you provide evidence of progress toward full compliance."

The gospel parallel to the positive incentive logic is really quite wonderful. God recognizes that an interim period will be required before most can comply fully with any one of his laws. Baptism takes care of past mistakes and signals the beginning of a period of learning and change. As we repent and partake of the sacrament on a weekly basis, we find that our transition period mistakes are forgiven as long as the Holy Ghost (internal auditor) certifies that we are sincere in our attempt to make progress toward full compliance.

What about a gospel "grandfather clause"? Is there some way that any of us can continue on in our old ways and be exempted from laws and penalties that apply to others? I suspect the reader knows the answer. The grandfather-clause solution in secular situations usually arises out of a need for political or economic compromise. The regulating entity would prefer full compliance but the regulated entity has enough political or economic power to make it difficult or impossible to achieve the desired result. Thus, in order to make as much progress as possible, the regulator requires full compliance from all but those few who have the political or economic power to success-fully resist. After much negotiation and discussion the few are "grandfathered" in or are allowed to operate in their old ways without sanctions being imposed.

It should come as no surprise that God is in a position where it is neither necessary nor desirable for him to compromise his laws. In Alma 42:25 we read, "What, do you suppose that mercy can rob justice? I say unto you, Nay; not one whit. If so, God would cease to be God."

God cannot and will not require compliance of some people and not of others. It's not in the plan!

SATISFYING THE LAW

Let us consider more carefully how the process of justifica-tion prepares us to return again to the presence of our Heavenly Father. We know we must be perfected and cleansed from sin if we would dwell again with God: "Neither can filthiness or any-thing which is unclean be received into the kingdom of God" (Alma 7:21). We must meet the standard of perfect exactness in the fulfillment or satisfying of the law. How can this be done?

Satisfying the law can be accomplished by any one of three

ways or by some combination of all three together. The three possibilities are:

First, to perfectly abide by the law.

Second, to repent of the parts of the law that have been broken and are to be covered by the atoning blood of Christ.

Third, to suffer or personally pay the penalty for any portion of the law that was broken and unrepented of.

FIRST: ABIDING THE LAW

God's laws or commandments are set with the object of perfecting his children that they might be able to return to his presence. A person may be justified vis à vis a particular law by exactly keeping or abiding by that law. In such a case it may be said that the law has no claim on the person. However, when a law is *not* kept it *does* have a claim on the person in the form of a penalty that must be paid for breaking the law. Saying that the law has claim on a person is another way of saying that the individual has an outstanding debt in the form of an unpaid penalty. The Holy Ghost, as earlier discussed, certifies if a person indeed has kept a law exactly and therefore warrants that no penalty needs to be paid and no debt needs to be discharged.

The scriptures teach us that this is an unlikely path to perfection. In Romans 3:20 we read, "Therefore by the deeds of the law there shall no flesh be justified in his sight: for by the law is the knowledge of sin." And 2 Nephi 2:5 reads, "And men are instructed sufficiently that they know good from evil. And the law is given unto men. And by the law no flesh is justified."

These verses both express the same central concept: no

one's actions (deeds) will meet the exacting standards of the law fully enough to warrant complete justification. Only one person has lived his life in such a way that the Holy Ghost could warrant that every law was kept exactly. That person, of course, is Jesus Christ, the Son of God. It can be said of him that the law has no claim on him. For Christ, there are no penalties to be paid because there was not even one instance where the law was broken.

For everyone else who has ever lived, there will have been infractions of the law that prevent the Holy Ghost from certifying the person free from sin. Thus, when measured by the exacting standards of the law, "no flesh is [or can be] justified," or no person will be certified as having met the standard of exactness required for justification of the whole law.

Second: Satisfying the Law through Repentance

The Apostle Paul states, "For all have sinned, and come short of the glory of God" (Romans 3:23). Because no one will be able to completely keep the whole law, it is fortunate that there is a second possibility for satisfying the law. Alma alerts us to this possibility when he says, "There is a law given, and a punishment affixed, and a repentance granted" (Alma 42:22). Mormon explains, "For repentance is unto them that are under condemnation and under the curse of a broken law" (Moroni 8:24). Thus, a person who has not completely lived a law and would therefore be "under the curse of a broken law" can choose to meet the demands of justice by invoking the principle of repentance.

God has provided that the penalty which must accompany any broken law can be paid by his Son, Jesus Christ, upon condition of our repentance. Helaman explains that the power to redeem is given to Christ by his Father: "The Lord surely should come to redeem his people, but . . . he should not come to redeem them in their sins, but to redeem them from their sins. And he hath *power given unto him from the Father* to redeem . . . ; therefore he hath sent his angels to declare the tidings of the *conditions* of repentance, which bringeth unto the power of the Redeemer, unto the salvation of their souls" (Helaman 5:10–11; emphasis added).

God the Father has given his Son the power to redeem his people "from their sins *because of repentance*," or *through the principle of repentance* (Helaman 5:11; emphasis added). Those that elect the option to satisfy the law through repentance can expect that the demands of justice will be satisfied by the atoning blood of Christ. As Lehi says, "Wherefore, redemption cometh in and through the Holy Messiah; for he is full of grace and truth. Behold he offereth himself a sacrifice for sin, to answer the ends of the law, unto all those who have a broken heart and a contrite spirit; and unto none else can the ends of the law be answered" (2 Nephi 2:6–7).

With repentance, the Holy Ghost is again involved in the justification process by verifying that the conditions of repentance have been met and that the "ends of the law" can be answered by the atonement. Without such a certification, the repentance process is not complete and cannot be counted on to satisfy the demands of justice. Of course, the Holy Ghost assists in the process in another way. He not only observes our efforts but because of our faith in Christ, the Holy Ghost actively helps us along the way.

THIRD: SATISFYING THE LAW THROUGH PERSONAL SUFFERING

There is a third possibility for satisfying the demands of the law. The person who has not kept the law and will not repent must pay the penalty through personal suffering. The Lord has said, "But if they would not repent they must suffer even as I; which suffering caused myself, even God, the greatest of all, to tremble because of pain, and to bleed at every pore, and to suffer both body and spirit" (D&C 19:17–18). Clearly, personal suffering for one's sins is far and away the least attractive option for satisfying the demands of the law. It is also clear that if the law is not lived or repented of, there is no recourse but to experience the pain and suffering described by the Lord.

Today in modern jurisprudence there are sentencing guidelines that spell out the penalty one can expect to pay for each kind of law that is broken. The penalties range from home confinement and fines to lengthy prison sentences or even execution. While the nature and duration of God's punishments have not been spelled out, he has provided some insight into the matter. He has declared, "And surely every man must repent or suffer, for I, God, am endless. . . . Nevertheless, it is not written that there shall be no end to this torment, but it is written *endless torment. . . .* For, behold, I am endless, and the punishment which is given from my hand is endless punishment, for Endless is my name. Wherefore—Eternal punishment is God's punishment. Endless punishment is God's punishment" (D&C 19:4, 6, 10–12).

Though God does not provide specific sentencing guidelines, it is a safe assumption that "God's punishment" will be carefully designed and carried out. Alma states, "Justice claimeth the creature and executeth the law, and the law inflicteth the punishment; if not so, the works of justice would be destroyed, and God would cease to be God" (Alma 42:22).

Because God has established a system of laws and punishments that cannot be altered or "God would cease to be God," there seem to be only two ways for God to encourage his children to comply.

A HORRIBLE APPROACH

We are given an insight into one approach in the previously cited scripture from the Doctrine and Covenants. God states, "It is written *endless torment.* Again, it is written *eternal damnation; wherefore it is more express than other scriptures, that it might work upon the hearts of the children of men, altogether for my name's glory*" (D&C 19:6–7).

If personal suffering for unrepented sins is clearly avoidable, and if the suffering will be truly horrible, then a loving God who would wish to have his children avoid such suffering would want to paint the picture in language as strong as possible. The phrases *a lake of fire and brimstone, eternal damnation,* and *endless torment* are explicitly calculated to "work upon the hearts of the children of men, altogether for my name's glory." God has made it clear that his work and glory is "to bring to pass the immortality and eternal life of man" (Moses 1:39). God does not glory in the punishment of man, but desires to provide all the encouragement possible for man to avoid punishment and be exalted. When God's words work upon men's hearts, and those hearts are changed, the resulting blessings are indeed to his name's glory.

THE HEAVENLY APPROACH

Painting the horrible picture of personal suffering is necessary and represents "fair disclosure," but the scriptures make it abundantly evident that a loving Heavenly Father prefers an alternative approach. The "heavenly" approach is to explain the principles of repentance and atonement and to encourage men in every way to take advantage of the blessings of exaltation that come from satisfying the law through repentance. God is untiring in his efforts to provide encouragement, exhortation, and motivation of every kind, that man might choose repentance and Christ's atonement as the means whereby the demands of the law are satisfied.

One of the clearest and most consistent themes in all of scripture is repentance. The exhortation to repent has been sounded by prophets of every dispensation. The Prophet Joseph Smith and his contemporaries were repeatedly told by the Lord to "say nothing but repentance unto this generation" (D&C 6:9; 11:9; 14:8; 19:21). These exhortations come from a loving

Father who knows that the demands of justice will be met. He knows also that his Son has suffered for men so they might not suffer if they would repent. He therefore provides constant encouragement that we might each choose the heavenly approach to justification.

THE PROCESS OF JUSTIFICATION

To further understand the process of justification, consider the diagram in figure 14. The law in its entirety is represented

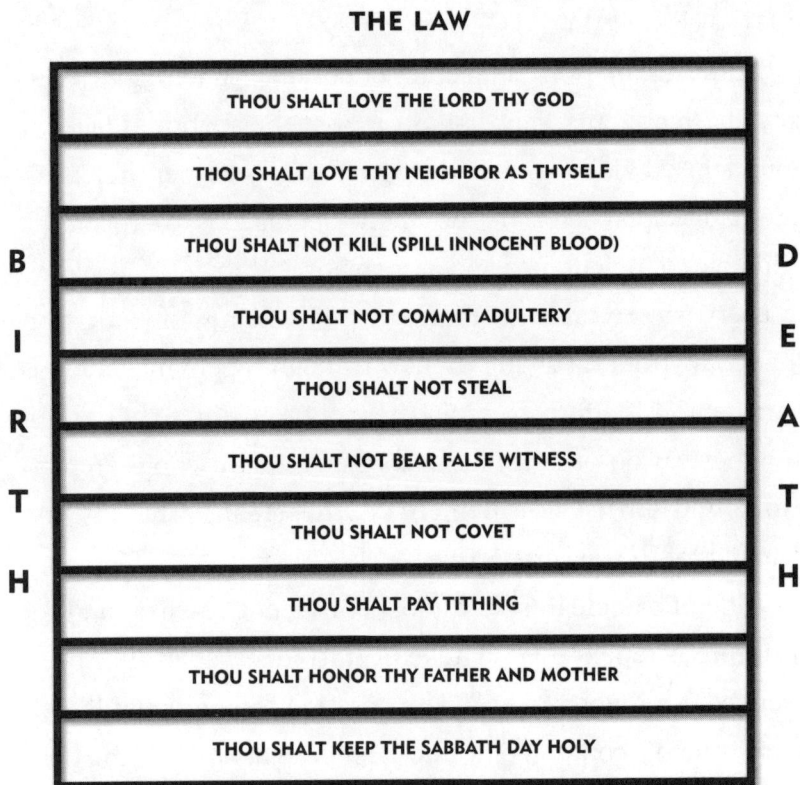

THE LAW

B
I
R
T
H

| THOU SHALT LOVE THE LORD THY GOD |
| THOU SHALT LOVE THY NEIGHBOR AS THYSELF |
| THOU SHALT NOT KILL (SPILL INNOCENT BLOOD) |
| THOU SHALT NOT COMMIT ADULTERY |
| THOU SHALT NOT STEAL |
| THOU SHALT NOT BEAR FALSE WITNESS |
| THOU SHALT NOT COVET |
| THOU SHALT PAY TITHING |
| THOU SHALT HONOR THY FATHER AND MOTHER |
| THOU SHALT KEEP THE SABBATH DAY HOLY |

D
E
A
T
H

Figure 14

by the whole rectangle. The rectangle is bounded on the left-hand side by birth and the right-hand side by death, indicating the boundaries of our experience with the law. From top to bottom is a partial listing of individual commandments or injunctions which, when combined together, constitute the law. The area in each horizontal bar represents one's entire life experience with the commandment in question.

As an illustration of how each of us must be perfect in fulfilling the law, consider the commandment "Thou shalt not steal." Ultimately it will be necessary to completely satisfy the law in one or more of the three possible ways previously discussed. First, it may be that a person could keep the law perfectly by never having stolen anything in his or her lifetime. In this case the Holy Ghost warrants that the law was perfectly kept. Let us represent that possibility with a horizontal bar shaded light gray, as in figure 15.

THOU SHALT NOT STEAL

Figure 15

A second possibility is that the law was mostly kept, but at some time the law was broken—something was stolen. This sin was subsequently repented of, and the repentance was justified by the Holy Ghost to have been carried out correctly. In this instance, part of the law would be fulfilled by the atonement of the Savior. Figure 16 depicts this possibility with a bar that is

97

mostly light gray but has some part shaded medium gray, representing that part of the law covered by the atonement.

THOU SHALT NOT STEAL

Figure 16

A third possibility is that some part of the law was kept, some part was broken and repented of, and some part was broken without accompanying repentance. To fulfill the law, the penalty for the part that was not repented of could not be covered by the atonement and would have to be paid by the individual. Figure 17 depicts this case shading a portion of the bar light gray, a portion medium gray, and a portion dark gray.

THOU SHALT NOT STEAL

Figure 17

The amount of light, medium, or dark gray on any bar will vary from individual to individual and from law to law, depending on how a person lives his or her life. For example, for the vast majority of individuals the bar labeled "Thou shalt not kill" will be completely shaded light gray, signifying that the commandment was kept throughout their lives because no innocent blood was ever shed. Other bars representing commandments may be completely shaded medium gray or completely shaded dark gray. What is clear is that the whole law must be completely satisfied for every individual. How much of the law is obeyed (light gray), repented of and atoned for (medium gray), or suffered for by the individual (dark gray) will vary on an individual basis according to personal righteousness and attention to the principle of repentance. In the final analysis, an individual profile will have a mix of "shadings" that represent the person's life and justification by the law. Figure 18 illustrates one possible profile.

JUSTIFICATION PROFILE

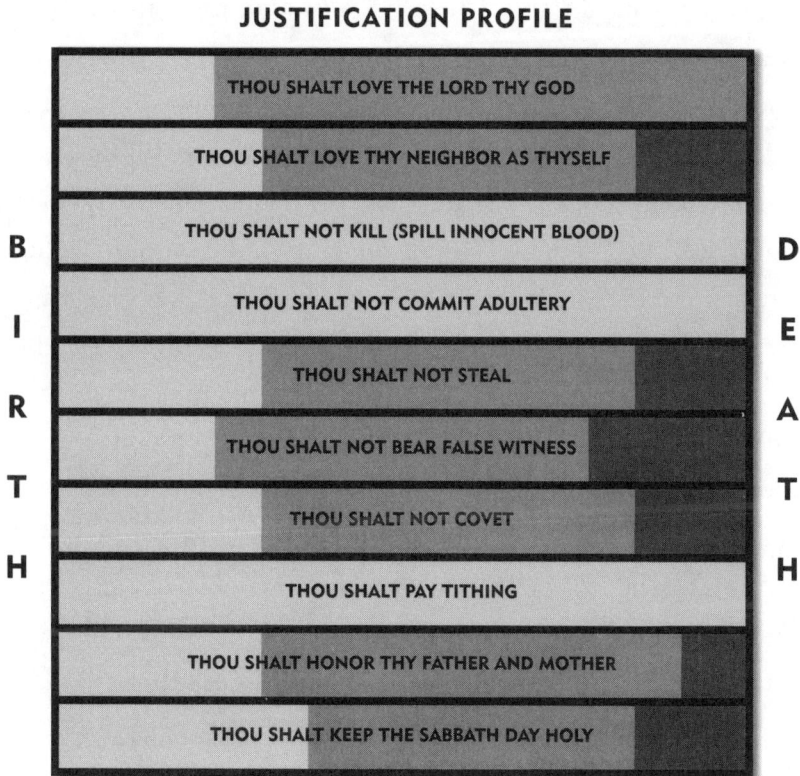

Figure 18

We must understand that while we do not control the process of justification we *do* control the critical decision of how the process will impact our lives and the outcomes we will have. How much of our "profile" is shaded light, medium, or dark gray is very much up to us.

I was recently impressed at how quickly this notion was grasped by a group of young people with whom I was speaking. After discussing the concept of justification in general and explaining how the demands of the law may be met, we looked together at a diagram similar to figure 18. We talked about what the patterns meant and then spent several minutes focusing on the personal suffering that would come to those who experienced the dark gray part of the diagram. Some moments of quiet reflection passed as each person pondered how this concept might have application in his or her life. Finally one young man observed in a subdued tone of humility and reverence, "So, Brother Nadauld, the idea is to extend the medium gray zone, right?" Without intending any disrespect but using terms he could understand, the young man stated his realization that he would be infinitely better off if he were able to substitute the medium gray shading, representing the atonement and mercy of the Savior, for the dark gray section, representing personal suffering. We then had a very meaningful discussion about obedience and the importance of repentance in a context that allowed those young people to fully understand the potential consequences of their behavior.

SELF-JUSTIFICATION

To avoid the punishment affixed to broken laws, we must qualify for the atonement. That is why it is so important that consideration be given to the concept of *self-justification*. Self-justification occurs when we act as our own compliance officers. At an elementary level, the problem with this approach is rather obvious. We have previously mentioned the possibility of looking at a word and pronouncing it spelled correctly "according to me." If we are wrong, we lose points on the spelling exam or English paper or possibly look foolish to our boss. After a while we learn to consult the dictionary in order to comply with accepted spelling standards and avoid the problems that accompany our incorrect self-assessment.

Similar arguments could be made with respect to the preparation of tax returns. In fact, this is recognized as more tenuous terrain, and most seek expert advice rather than risk serving as their own auditors and making a mistake that would have serious financial or criminal penalties. We somehow intuitively recognize that it would be unwise to serve as our own compliance officers where expert help is readily available and the penalties for noncompliance are onerous. Unfortunately, that same wisdom does not always accompany our behavior relative to God's laws.

It is a common thing for us to justify our own behavior. We usually feel we are in the best position to judge the correctness of our actions in regard to the law. We reason that we know the facts, circumstances, pressures, and nuances that have led to our actions. Even though experience teaches that we are not always objective in our assessments, we become resentful when others question our objectivity or point out our shortcomings. These mental and emotional struggles are familiar to every entrant into life's arena.

This inability or unwillingness to be objective about our own behavior is generally rooted in what the scriptures refer to as "the pride of their hearts" (2 Nephi 28:15; Jacob 2:13; Alma 1:6; Helaman 13:27; Mormon 8:28, 36). Prophets ancient and modern have recognized pride, or the self-assessment of one's own value, to be man's greatest single shortcoming.

Mormon, by virtue of editing so much history of his people, was able to offer a classic insight into these matters. After reviewing nearly four hundred years of history, he observed in Helaman 12: "O how foolish, and how vain, and how evil, and devilish, and how quick to do iniquity, and how slow to do good, are the children of men; yea, how quick to hearken unto the words of the evil one, and to set their hearts upon the vain things of the world!

"Yea, how quick to be lifted up in pride; yea, how quick to boast, and do all manner of that which is iniquity; and how slow are they to remember the Lord their God, and to give ear unto his counsels, yea, how slow to walk in wisdom's paths!

"Behold, they do not desire that the Lord their God, who hath created them, should rule and reign over them; notwithstanding his great goodness and his mercy towards them, they do set at naught his counsels, and they will not that he should be their guide.

"O how great is the nothingness of the children of men; yea, even they are less than the dust of the earth. For behold, the dust of the earth moveth hither and thither, to the dividing asunder, at the command of our great and everlasting God" (Helaman 12:4–8).

The implication in the vernacular is that men are "dumber than dirt"! Mormon points out that at least the dust of the earth responds to God's commands but men "set at naught his counsels, and . . . will not that he should be their guide."

If pride and the accompanying self-justification led only to the inevitable result of making us look foolish, it would be bad enough. But that's the least of the problems. The business of acting as one's own compliance officer has extremely serious consequences.

These consequences arise when we deem ourselves to be in compliance with a law or commandment and we are wrong in our assessment. God will look to the Holy Ghost—not us—to certify our compliance with the law. That is the very essence of the phrase *by the Spirit ye are justified*. Punishment for noncompliance will be meted out based on the report *given by the Holy Ghost*. To see how serious it is to be wrong in our self-justification we need only read Doctrine and Covenants 19:16–18: "For behold I, God, have suffered these things for all, that they might not suffer if they would repent; but if they would not repent they must suffer even as I; which suffering caused myself, even God, the greatest of all, to tremble because of pain, and to bleed at every pore, and to suffer both body and spirit."

The problem with self-justification is obvious. If we believe we are in compliance and our assessment is incorrect we will have lost the opportunity to repent. Having lost that opportunity we will have to suffer the intense pain and agony that accompany our particular offenses. This is the real problem with pride. *The trouble is not so much that pride is an ungraceful trait but that it prevents us from accessing the blessings of the atonement.*

Thank heaven for the gift of the Holy Ghost! If we are willing to listen to the promptings of the Spirit we can be made aware of the changes that need to be made. It is quite clear that our shortcomings will not be "glossed over." This is true despite specious arguments to the contrary. There is a classic line in the Book of Mormon illustrating a time-tested but false logic. We read in 2 Nephi 28:8: "And there shall also be many which shall say: Eat, drink, and be merry; nevertheless, fear God—he will *justify* in committing a little sin; yea, lie a little, take the advantage of one because of his words, dig a pit for thy neighbor, there is no harm in this; and do all these things, for tomorrow we die; and if it so be that we are guilty, God will beat us with a few stripes, and at last we shall be saved in the kingdom of God."

This logic has appeal to those who wish to think of God as someone who will overlook the fuzziness at the edges of their behavior. While the logic is appealing, it is both misleading (as the devil hoped it would be) and completely incorrect. The demands of the law *will* be met, either through our own efforts or by the atonement of Jesus Christ. If we choose to partake of the blessings of the atonement through repentance, the Holy Ghost knows whether or not we have done it sincerely and completely. He will then certify whether or not the penalty we might have suffered will be covered by the atoning blood of the Savior.

The bishop's assignment as a common judge is to assist us in the repentance process. It is wholly to our advantage to be completely truthful and forthcoming. But the bishop, even with the power of discernment, may or may not be prompted that something is not quite right. On the other hand, the Holy Ghost will know perfectly, and it is his certification of exactness that will be accepted in the final analysis.

This principle—that the Holy Ghost will certify whether or not we merit the atoning blood of the Savior—provides a ready answer to the false logic of planned repentance. We cannot with premeditation plan to sin and simultaneously plan to repent. The principle of repentance requires true and unmanipulated contrition. God will not be mocked, nor will he allow the atoning sacrifice of his Son to be applied without merit. The full implication of "by the Spirit ye are justified, and by the blood ye are sanctified" must be understood by all who would have claim on the mercy and grace of Jesus Christ.

JUSTIFICATION: A NECESSARY BUT NOT SUFFICIENT CONDITION FOR EXALTATION

Our discussion of justification has led us to understand that every individual will have to satisfy the law by (1) complete obedience, (2) forgiveness through the atonement, or (3) personal suffering. All will have to be justified, or found to be in compliance with the laws of God. Since all will *eventually* meet the demands of the law one way or another, it could be supposed that all of God's children would *finally* find themselves together in the same kingdom. Is that to be the case? Is the only consequence to unrepented sin the personal suffering that must be endured?

Consider for a moment the notion of "necessary but not sufficient." In mathematics, the phrase is often employed with regard to the proof of a proposition or theorem. The concept is that a particular condition is *necessary* for a theorem to be true but by itself it is not enough or *sufficient* to satisfy the complete requirements for proof. Similarly, it is true that justification is *necessary* for salvation, but alone it is not a *sufficient* condition for exaltation in the highest kingdom available to those who are "saved." It is only one of several requirements the Lord has given us.

That justification is a necessary but not sufficient condition for ultimate salvation is confirmed in Doctrine and Covenants 76. Here it is clearly revealed that there are categories or gradations of conditions and outcomes corresponding to the rewards or penalties we receive after this life.

About this section of the Doctrine and Covenants the Prophet wrote, "Upon my return from Amherst conference, I resumed the translation of the Scriptures. From sundry revelations which had been received, it was apparent that many important points touching the salvation of man had been taken from the Bible, or lost before it was compiled. It appeared self-evident from what truths were left, that if God rewarded every one according to deeds done in the body, the term 'Heaven,' as intended for the Saints' eternal home, must include *more kingdoms than one*" (D&C 76, head note; emphasis added). As the Prophet considered these issues, he and Sidney Rigdon received the revelation recorded in Doctrine and Covenants 76.

In that vision the Prophet explains that "while we were doing the work of translation, which the Lord had appointed to us, we came to the twenty-ninth verse of the fifth chapter of John, which was given unto us as follows—Speaking of the resurrection of the dead, concerning those who shall hear the voice of the Son of Man: and shall come forth; they who have done good, in the resurrection of the just; and they who have done evil, in the resurrection of the unjust" (D&C 76:15–17).

The Prophet further explains, "While we meditated upon these things, the Lord touched the eyes of our understandings and they were opened" (D&C 76:19). What immediately followed was a revelation of the two extremes they read of in John—the resurrection of the just and of the unjust. The Prophet was shown the Only Begotten of the Father sitting on the right hand of God. He also saw an angel of God who had rebelled against the Only Begotten Son "and was called Perdition, for the heavens wept over him—he was Lucifer, a son of the morning" (D&C 76:26). The vision then set forth for the Prophet's understanding the conditions and outcomes attached to the two ends of the spectrum of human behavior.

The first set of conditions enumerated pertain to the "sons of perdition," those who will receive no salvation whatsoever and who are described as "the only ones who shall not be redeemed in the due time of the Lord" (D&C 76:38). It is very instructive to sort through the text of the revelation and group all the conditions of perdition together in one listing, followed by the outcomes grouped together in a separate listing.

PERDITION: CONDITIONS AND OUTCOMES

CONDITIONS
1. Know God's power, v. 31
2. Have been made partakers thereof, v. 31
3. Suffered themselves through the power of the devil to be overcome, v. 31
4. Deny the truth, v. 31
5. Defy God's power, v. 31
6. Deny the Holy Spirit after receiving it, v. 35
7. Deny the Only Begotten of the Father, v. 35
8. Crucify him unto themselves and put him to open shame, v. 35

OUTCOMES
1. Are called sons of perdition, v. 32
2. No forgiveness in this world nor in the world to come, v. 34
3. Go away into the lake of fire and brimstone, with the devil and his angels, v. 36
4. The only ones on whom the second death shall have any power, v. 37
5. The only ones who shall not be redeemed in the due time of the Lord, after the sufferings of his wrath, v. 38

6. Shall go away into everlasting punishment, which is end-less punishment, which is eternal punishment, v. 44

7. The end thereof, neither the place thereof, nor their torment, no man knows, except them who are made par-takers thereof, vv. 45, 46

Several important points can be made concerning the con-ditions and outcomes that characterize this "sons of perdition" category. First, the salient condition defining this category is not the *absence* of faith or belief in the Savior but the outright *rejec-tion* of the "Only Begotten of the Father" *after* having clearly known the power of the Lord and been made partakers of it. Though what constitutes "knowing" or "partaking" can be end-lessly debated, the results are nevertheless clear. The power of the atonement will *not* be extended to any who meet the con-ditions of outright denial and rejection.

Second, without the power of the atonement it is not possible to obtain forgiveness, and thus one of the outcomes is "no for-giveness in this world nor in the world to come." Without any possibility of forgiveness, individuals in this category will be left to satisfy the law through their own suffering. But it is worse than that! Because of the seriousness of their transgressions, it is not possible for them to ever be justified, and thus "they shall go away into everlasting punishment" and become "the only ones who shall *not be redeemed* in the due time of the Lord, after the sufferings of his wrath." The implication of this last state-ment is clear. *All* but those in this category will ultimately be redeemed ("saved" is a term often used by many Christian faiths), even though for some it will not be until "after the sufferings of his wrath." The picture painted for those who choose to be "vessels of wrath" is bleak indeed. For emphasis, the Lord exclaims, "I say that it had been better for them never to have been born."

By contrast, let us examine the conditions and outcomes that lie at the other end of the spectrum.

CELESTIAL CONDITIONS AND OUTCOMES

CONDITIONS

1. Received the testimony of Jesus, v. 51
2. Believed on his name, v. 51
3. Were baptized after manner of his burial [i.e., by immersion, with authority], v. 51
4. By keeping the commandments they are washed and cleansed from all their sins, v. 52
5. Receive the Holy Spirit, v. 52
6. Overcome by faith, v. 53
7. Are sealed by the Holy Spirit of promise, v. 53

OUTCOMES

1. Are the church of the Firstborn, v. 54
2. Are they into whose hands the Father has given all things, v. 55
3. Are priests and kings, who have received of his fulness, and of his glory, v. 56

4. Are priests of the Most High, after the order of Melchizedek, v. 57

5. Are gods, even the *sons of God*, v. 58

6. All things are theirs, v. 59

7. Are Christ's, v. 59

8. Shall overcome all things, v. 60

9. Shall dwell in the presence of God and his Christ forever, v. 62

10. Shall come with Christ, when he shall come in the clouds of heaven to reign on the earth over his people, v. 63

11. Shall have part in the first resurrection, v. 64

12. Shall come forth in the resurrection of the just, v. 65

13. Are come unto Mount Zion, v. 66

14. Have come to an innumerable company of angels, v. 67

15. Their names are written in heaven, v. 68

16. Are just [i.e., *justified*] men made perfect through Jesus, v. 69

17. Are they whose bodies are celestial, v. 70

Foremost among celestial conditions is receiving the testimony of Jesus and believing on his name. Individuals at this end of the spectrum are characterized by their complete acceptance of the Savior and their willingness to be baptized, receive the Holy Spirit, and keep the commandments, that "they might be washed and cleansed from all their sins." Again we see that the salient condition is one's attitude toward the Only Begotten of the Father.

It is also interesting to note the role of the Holy Spirit or Holy Ghost. One of the perdition conditions is denial of the Holy Spirit, as contrasted to the celestial condition of acceptance or receipt of the Holy Spirit. This is consistent with the scriptures' teaching that "by the Spirit ye are justified" and the companion notion that the Holy Ghost is a heavenly compliance officer. In other words, those who accept the promptings of the Holy Ghost and repent will have their sins washed clean by the atoning blood of the Savior and can be warranted by the Holy Ghost as being in compliance with the law and justified *without* having to personally suffer for their sins.

One among many of the happy outcomes is that having thus been *justified* they "shall come forth in the resurrection of the *just*" (emphasis added) and "shall have part in the first resurrection." An individual who has been justified by living the law, coupled with repentance when necessary, avoids personally suffering for his sins. Because no time is lost in personally suffering for his sins, the individual is justified and ready for the *first* resurrection and the celestial kingdom.

After showing the Prophet Joseph the two ends of the spectrum, the Lord revealed two other categories and sets of conditions. These conditions pertain to kingdoms designated as terrestrial and telestial.

TERRESTRIAL CONDITIONS AND OUTCOMES

CONDITIONS

1. Died without law, v. 72
2. Spirits of men kept in prison, whom the Son visited, and to whom he preached the gospel, v. 73
3. Received not the testimony of Jesus in the flesh, but afterwards received it, v. 74
4. Not valiant in the testimony of Jesus, v. 79
5. Honorable men of the earth blinded by the craftiness of men, v. 75

OUTCOMES

1. Receive of his glory, but not of his fulness, v. 76
2. Receive of the presence of the Son, but *not* of the fulness of the Father, v. 77
3. Are bodies terrestrial, v. 78
4. Obtain not the crown over the kingdom of our God, v. 79

As in the previous two categories, the central defining conditions for this kingdom concern acceptance of Jesus Christ as the Savior. Those in this category "received not the testimony of Jesus in the flesh, but afterwards received it" or were "not valiant in the testimony of Jesus." The implication is that a witness was given, but the person refused to accept the gospel. A person who had a chance to receive the gospel but did not do so would be in much the same circumstance as one who was not valiant in a testimony received. In both cases the result would be an inability to take advantage of repentance and the atonement in this mortal sphere.

That these individuals comprise the honorable men of the earth suggests they would be in compliance with many of the laws of God. Nevertheless, they would have some sins that they had not repented of in this life and that would therefore not be covered by the atonement. They would have to repent of these things after they heard the gospel and received a testimony of the Savior in the next life. Thus it would *not* be possible for them to be justified before forfeiting some of the blessings promised to those who were valiant in their testimony of the Savior while in mortality. Their ultimate reward is described as receiving the glory and presence "of the Son but *not* the fulness of the Father." Thus they "obtain not the crown over the kingdom of our God."

Telestial Conditions and Outcomes

CONDITIONS

1. Received not the gospel of Christ, v. 82
2. Received not the testimony of Jesus, v. 82
3. Deny not the Holy Spirit, v. 83
4. Received not the prophets, v. 101
5. Received not the everlasting covenant, v. 101
6. Are liars, and sorcerers, and adulterers, and whoremongers, v. 103

OUTCOMES

1. Are thrust down to hell, v. 84
2. Are not redeemed from the devil until the last resurrection, v. 85
3. Receive not of his fulness in the eternal world, but of the Holy Spirit through the ministration of the terrestrial, v. 86
4. Suffer the wrath of God on earth, v. 104
5. Suffer the vengeance of eternal fire, v. 105
6. Suffer wrath of Almighty God, until the fulness of times, v. 106
7. Are innumerable as the stars in the heaven, or as the sand upon the seashore, v. 109
8. Will not be gathered with the saints, to be caught up unto the church of the Firstborn, and received into the cloud, v. 102

This category contains those individuals who are not willing to accept the Savior, his teachings, his covenants, or his prophets; however, unlike the sons of perdition, they do *not* deny the Holy Spirit. Further, their *evil works* distinguished them from those in the terrestrial kingdom, who are at least described as the honorable men of the earth. Because telestial beings deny the Savior and therefore cannot have their sins forgiven, and because they have so much to be forgiven for, they "shall not be redeemed from the devil until the last resurrection" (v. 25). They will have to pay for their own sins, and they will "suffer the wrath of Almighty God until the fulness of times."

Reviewing the conditions associated with each of the four defined categories (the three degrees of glory plus the state of perdition) reveals three broad groups of characteristic conditions that differentiate one kingdom from another: (1) attitude

	ATTITUDE TOWARD THE SAVIOR	ACCEPT OR REJECT THE HOLY GHOST	PERSONAL WORKS
CELESTIAL	Receive the testimony of Jesus Believe on His name	Receive the Holy Ghost Sealed by the Holy Spirit of Promise	Keep the commandments
TERRESTRIAL	Receive not the testimony of Jesus in the flesh Not valiant in the testimony of Jesus	(not stated)	Live honorable lives
TELESTIAL	Receive not the testimony of Jesus Receive not His teachings (the gospel) Receive not His prophets Receive not the everlasting covenant	Deny *not* the Holy Ghost	Liars, sorcerers, adulterers, and whoremongers
SONS OF PERDITION	Deny the Only Begotten of the Father Crucify Him unto themselves and put Him to open shame Defy "my power"	Deny the Holy Ghost after receiving it	Suffer themselves through the power of the devil to be overcome Deny the truth

Table 1

toward the Savior, (2) acceptance of the Holy Ghost, and (3) personal works (see table 1).

As we have observed, the central defining characteristic that separates individuals of one kingdom from those of another is attitude toward the Savior. This attitude ranges from complete acceptance by those in the celestial kingdom to complete rejection by those in the sons of perdition category. In fact, those in the sons of perdition category appear to go past complete rejection and on to defiance and rebellion as they "crucify him unto themselves and put him to open shame." (D&C 76:35). The summary of Table 1 also underscores two other serious considerations: first, the importance of our acceptance of the Holy Ghost; and second, the critical nature of our personal works.

We can see from this analysis that *personal works do matter!* And not only do works matter, but so do rites. The gospel of Jesus Christ includes rites and ordinances such as baptism, bestowal of the Holy Ghost, priesthood ordinations, and temple ordinances that must be experienced to prepare one for exaltation in the kingdom of God.

Justification is indeed a necessary but not sufficient condition for exaltation. All who inherit the celestial kingdom will have to have been justified by the Spirit. Other conditions for exaltation include: (1) complete belief in and acceptance of Jesus Christ as Savior and Redeemer, (2) acceptance of the Holy Ghost, and (3) righteous personal works, including the rites and ordinances of the gospel and sealing power of the temple ordinances.

Thus, all who inherit any kingdom of glory will have to

have satisfied the law in one way or another, but not all who are justified will inherit the celestial or highest kingdom of glory.

TWO SPECIAL PROVISIONS

We have examined the conditions and outcomes associated with the three categories, or degrees, of glory and one of darkness spelled out in Doctrine and Covenants 76. There are two additional provisions for special cases that the Lord revealed to the Prophet Joseph Smith. The first of these provisions came to the Prophet's attention in January of 1836 in the Kirtland Temple. After being given a glimpse of the celestial kingdom Joseph stated, "I saw Father Adam and Abraham; and my father and my mother; my brother Alvin, that has long since slept; and marveled how it was that he had obtained an inheritance in that kingdom, seeing that he had departed this life before the Lord had set his hand to gather Israel the second time, and had not been baptized for the remission of sins.

"Thus came the voice of the Lord unto me, saying: All who have died without a knowledge of this gospel, who would have received it if they had been permitted to tarry, shall be heirs of the celestial kingdom of God; also all that shall die henceforth without a knowledge of it, who would have received it *with all their hearts*, shall be heirs of that kingdom; for I, the Lord, will judge all men according to their works, *according to the desire of their hearts*" (D&C 137:5–9; emphasis added).

Since all who die without a knowledge of the gospel will inherit the *celestial* kingdom *if* they would have received it *with all their hearts*, we must infer that those who inherit the *terrestrial* kingdom "who died without law" (D&C 76:72) are those who would *not* have received the gospel with all their hearts.

The second special provision was revealed to the Prophet in the same vision. We read, "And I also beheld that all children who die before they arrive at the years of accountability are saved in the celestial kingdom of heaven" (D&C 137:10).

In an earlier dispensation the prophet Mormon commented on this issue: "If I have learned the truth, there have been disputations among you concerning the baptism of your little children. . . . Immediately after I had learned these things of you I inquired of the Lord concerning the matter. And the word of the Lord came to me by the power of the Holy Ghost, saying: . . .

"Wherefore, little children are whole, for they are not capable of committing sin; wherefore the curse of Adam is taken from them in me, that it hath no power over them" (Moroni 8:5–8).

Mormon was clearly given to understand that little children are not able to commit sin and that they are "alive in Christ" (Moroni 8:12) and "partakers of salvation" (Moroni 8:17). As we have learned, Joseph further clarified this doctrine for us in our dispensation, as our understanding of salvation was extended to include multiple kingdoms and it was made clear that salvation for little children meant an inheritance in the celestial kingdom.

Mormon also spoke of those who die without the law. He observed, "For behold that all little children are alive in Christ, and also all they that are without the law. For the power of redemption cometh on all them that have no law" (Moroni 8:22).

These two special provisions, together with the conditions and outcomes previously discussed, underscore further the proposition that justification is a necessary but not sufficient condition for reaching the highest of our Heavenly Father's kingdoms. Indeed, all who enter any of God's kingdoms of glory will have to have experienced the process of justification, but our ultimate happiness will also depend on our attitude toward the Savior, our acceptance of the Holy Ghost, our works, and whether we fall under either of the two special categories.

JUSTIFIED BY FAITH

It is only by having faith in Christ and exercising that faith unto repentance that we can be justified, becoming free from the demands of justice. King Benjamin expresses this concept beautifully in his discourse found in Mosiah.

"And now, because of the covenant which ye have made ye shall be called the children of Christ, his sons, and his daughters; for behold, this day he hath spiritually begotten you; for ye say that *your hearts are changed through faith on his name*; therefore, ye are born of him and have become his sons and his daughters.

"*And under this head ye are made free, and there is no other head whereby ye can be made free. There is no other name given whereby salvation cometh*; therefore, I would that ye should take upon you the name of Christ, all you that have entered into the covenant with God that ye should be obedient unto the end of your lives" (Mosiah 5:7–8; emphasis added).

Faith in Christ causes a change of heart that leads to

repentance and freedom from the demands of justice. Those who accept Christ's sacrifice and repent and thereby merit his atoning blood will not have to suffer personally for their sins.

Those who have not faith or who reject Christ bring upon themselves the full force of the law and the horrible consequences spoken of in the scriptures. Jacob explains: "Behold, will ye reject these words? Will ye reject the words of the prophets; and will ye reject all the words which have been spoken concerning Christ, after so many have spoken concerning him; and deny the good word of Christ, and the power of God, and the gift of the Holy Ghost, and quench the Holy Spirit, and make a mock of the great plan of redemption, which hath been laid for you?

"Know ye not that if ye will do these things, that the power of the redemption and the resurrection, which is in Christ, will bring you to stand with shame and awful guilt before the bar of God? And according to the power of justice, for justice cannot be denied, ye must go away into that lake of fire and brimstone, whose flames are unquenchable, and whose smoke ascendeth up forever and ever, which lake of fire and brimstone is endless torment" (Jacob 6:8–10).

What sorrow for those who reject Christ and the Holy Ghost, and thereby "make a mock of the great plan of redemption"! Conversely, what joy and happiness await those who accept assurances and evidences, who develop faith in Christ and allow that faith to bless their lives! Surely we should give thanks for the grace of God.

5

---

*A*mazing
GRACE

"Amazing grace! How sweet the sound
That saved a wretch like me.
I once was lost but now am found,
Was blind, but now I see."

<small>TRADITIONAL HYMN</small>

To begin this last chapter, let us review the verses that have guided our study: "Therefore being *justified by faith*, we have peace with God through our Lord Jesus Christ: By whom also we have access by faith into this *grace* wherein we stand, and rejoice in hope of the glory of God" (Romans 5:1–2; emphasis added). We have defined faith and investigated at length the exacting process of justification. What should we now think of this *grace* to which Paul refers?

Consider the words and feeling in the traditional old gospel hymn, "Amazing Grace." They are a natural emollient to the perceived harshness of justice. *Amazing*—what a wonderful word! It seems to capture at once our humility, our awe and wonder, and the unbridled gratitude that should surely be associated with our understanding of grace. If justification seems analytical, our reaction to grace is more likely emotional. Indeed, there is such emotion and joy in contemplating the grace of the Savior that shouting "halleluia!" should seem natural.

It is possible to accept the logic and intellectual underpinnings of justification and still feel that it is a harsh doctrine. The love and understanding of caring parents who overlook faults may condition one to expect this special treatment in relation to eternal laws. Perhaps the sense of entitlement that seems more prevalent in our time also biases how justice and judgment are viewed. It is certainly not fashionable to take responsibility for one's actions and face the consequences. Most people have a a natural inclination to hope not that they will get what's coming to them, but that they will somehow get treated "well" or "preferentially."

But something very special happens when we fully appreciate the exacting nature of God's justice. When it becomes clear that we cannot wiggle around, talk our way through, or "schmooze" our way out of the consequences of our actions, when we have a realistic view of the perfectly exacting nature of the law, we are ready to begin to comprehend the extraordinary concept of grace: awesome, wonderful, amazing grace! Furthermore, not only is grace amazing when considered in relation to the law of justice, but it is equally wonderful in dealing with uncertainty, the other condition that must exist for us to make progress in this mortal sphere. In other words, as softening as grace is to the grim face of justice, it is equally soothing to the Janus faces of uncertainty. Indeed, to fully understand grace we must examine the notion of uncertainty.

EXASPERATING UNCERTAINTY

We may suppose that it is the uncertainty or the need for agency in life that makes us miserable. If we could only be sure that everything will turn out all right. Are we marrying the right person? Will we be able to make our mortgage payment? Will we get the promotion we want? What will happen with our children? What about our health, college tuition, retirement? The list goes on and on, and at the root of it all is that knotty problem of uncertainty! If we could just be in complete control and have things turn out exactly the way we want, think how the stresses of life would dissipate—think how happy we would be!

What could be wrong with a little more certainty? Nature enjoys certainty. Doesn't gravity work all the time? The sun comes up every day, spring follows winter, the rivers run, and the tides ebb and flow. The laws of physics and chemistry are deterministic and work the same way all the time, don't they? If we ignore the Heisenberg uncertainty principle, Einstein's theory of relativity, or chaos theory, most natural laws do appear to be tightly determined or certain.

We learn at an early age about certainty. We learn that fire will certainly burn, that if we jump off anything high we will certainly fall down, not up, and that the pain of landing will be related to the height of the fall. We learn that when we run into something we certainly get hurt, and that the hurt is related to the size of what we run into (or what runs into us). But we also learn about uncertainty. Some days we're happy and some days we're sad, we don't always get what we want for our birthdays, and sometimes bad things happen that aren't our fault.

It turns out that uncertainty is a necessary, even crucial element in our Heavenly Father's plan. To understand the role of uncertainty we need to remind ourselves of God's objective with us: "to bring to pass the immortality and eternal life of man" (Moses 1:39). To become like our Heavenly Father, we need to obtain knowledge and develop wisdom and judgment. We could not do this in an environment where every outcome was certain. We develop wisdom by observing and sorting between certain and uncertain outcomes. We develop judgment by choosing among uncertain possibilities and experiencing the consequences. In fact, wisdom and judgment have definition when uncertainty requires the exercise of agency. In a completely certain environment, there are no choices, hence no need for either wisdom or judgment. Every outcome is known in advance; there are no other possibilities.

President Spencer W. Kimball phrased these ideas in the following way: "Some become bitter when oft-repeated prayers seem unanswered. Some lose faith and turn sour when solemn administrations by holy men seem to be ignored and no restoration seems to come from repeated prayer circles. But if all the sick were healed, if all the righteous were protected and the wicked destroyed, the whole program of the Father would be annulled and the basic principle of the gospel, free agency, would be ended.

"If pain and sorrow and total punishment immediately followed the doing of evil, no soul would repeat a misdeed. If joy and peace and rewards were instantaneously given the doer of good, there could be no evil—all would do good and not because of the rightness of doing good. There would be no test of strength, no development of character, no growth of powers, no free agency. There would also be an absence of joy, success, resurrection, eternal life, and godhood" (*Teachings of Spencer W. Kimball,* ed. Edward L. Kimball, Salt Lake City: Bookcraft, 1982, 77).

Much to our occasional consternation, the development of character, the acquisition of spiritual power, and the realization of joy all require uncertainty.

UNCERTAINTY AND THE PARABLE OF THE TALENTS

The parable of the talents provides an interesting insight into the principle of uncertainty. We read, "For the kingdom of heaven is as a man travelling into a far country, who called his own servants, and delivered unto them his goods. And unto one he gave five talents, to another two, and to another one; to every man according to his several ability; and straightway took his journey.

"Then he that had received the five talents went and traded with the same, and made them other five talents. And likewise he that had received two, he also gained other two. But he that had received one went and digged in the earth, and hid his lord's money.

"After a long time the lord of those servants cometh, and reckoneth with them." At the reckoning, the servants with five talents and two talents both reported that they had doubled that which their lord had given them. The lord responded to each of them, "Well done, thou good and faithful servant: thou hast been faithful over a few things, *I will make thee ruler over many things: enter thou into the joy of thy lord.*"

"Then he which had received the one talent came and said, Lord, I knew thee that thou art an hard man, reaping where thou hast not sown, and gathering where thou hast not strawed: *And I was afraid,* and went and hid thy talent in the earth: lo, there thou hast that is thine. His lord answered and said unto him, Thou wicked and slothful servant, thou knewest that I reap where I sowed not, and gather where I have not strawed: Thou oughtest therefore to have put my money to the exchangers, and then at my coming I should have received mine own with usury.

"Take therefore the talent from him, and give it unto him which hath ten talents. For unto every one that hath shall be given, and he shall have abundance: but from him that hath not shall be taken away even that which he hath. And cast ye the unprofitable servant into outer darkness: there shall be weeping and gnashing of teeth" (Matthew 25:14–30; emphasis added).

Jesus begins this parable by drawing an analogy to *the kingdom of heaven*. In other words, he is teaching a principle that has universal application and is not limited to this earth only.

The principle of uncertainty is illustrated in this setting by comparing the outcomes and rewards associated with risky and riskless investments. It is clear that there was risk or uncertainty involved in both the five-talent and two-talent investments, or the third servant who "was afraid" would have also invested his one talent. But he did not. Because the servant feared an uncertain outcome, he hid the one talent in the earth and therefore was *certain* he could return it to the lord.

The servants that dealt wisely with uncertainty were told that they would be made rulers over many things and were invited to enter into the joy of the Lord. However, the servant that would not exercise judgment and because of fear sought for a riskless, certain outcome was told he was to be cast into outer darkness where there would be weeping and gnashing of teeth.

It is very interesting that the phrase "cast . . . into outer darkness" is employed in this context. Generally that phrase is used to describe the final state of the devil and his angels. For example, we read in Alma, "The spirits of the wicked, yea, who are evil—for behold, they have no part nor portion of the Spirit of the Lord; for behold, they chose evil works rather than good; therefore the spirit of the devil did enter into them, and take possession of their house–and these shall be *cast out into outer darkness*; there shall be weeping, and wailing, and gnashing of teeth, and this because of their own iniquity, being led captive by the will of the devil" (Alma 40:13). That a one-talent servant would be consigned to hell or outer darkness seems extreme—unless we take the view that such an outcome is less a result of his one slothful act and more an illustration of the principle that one who lives a life of complete certainty cannot develop the wisdom and judgment requisite for inheriting eternal life.

Actually, this is familiar gospel territory. In the premortal existence, in an effort to appeal to those who feared the unknown, the devil authored a plan that would eliminate uncertainty. Those who were unwilling to risk the judgments and uncertainty of this mortal experience will ultimately be cast into outer darkness, exactly as the parable of the talents suggests.

We read in Moses, "And I, the Lord God, spake unto Moses, saying: That Satan . . . is the same which was from the beginning, and he came before me, saying—Behold, here am I, send me, I will be thy son, and I will redeem all mankind, that one soul shall not be lost, and surely I will do it; wherefore give me thine honor.

"But, behold, my Beloved Son, which was my Beloved and Chosen from the beginning, said unto me—Father, thy will be done, and the glory be thine forever.

"Wherefore, because that Satan rebelled against me, and sought *to destroy the agency of man*, which I, the Lord God, had given him, and also, that I should give unto him mine own power; by the power of mine Only Begotten, I caused that he should be cast down" (Moses 4:1–3).

We generally think of the devil's plan as a plan of force, where everyone would be compelled to keep all the commandments all the time. This is just another way of describing a plan with certain outcomes. *Once provision is made for some outcome other than one that is certain or mandated, then the concepts of agency, choice, and uncertainty have meaning.*

It is quite remarkable how well we've learned to manage most aspects of uncertainty in our daily lives. We don't generally stop to quantify the level of uncertainty we face in day-to-day living, but as we develop wisdom and judgment, we act intuitively to reduce uncertainty to minimum or acceptable levels. For example, when considering whether or not to bungee jump off a bridge (which consideration we of course entertain frequently) most of us have the attitude that even if there's only one in a million odds that the bungee will break, there's no way I'm trusting that fool thing! We quickly learn to prudently manage all those uncertainties over which we have any control. We buy reasonable amounts of insurance, we don't gamble, we fasten our seat belts, and we assiduously avoid certain restaurants.

But there are two categories that bedevil us. There are judgment errors that accompany the learning process, and there are circumstances and outcomes over which we have little or no control. Errors in judgment, while inevitable, are nonetheless painful. Sometimes the learning errors affect only ourselves, though still they may be quite serious. But on other occasions, our mistakes not only cause anguish to our own souls, but result in great suffering or hardships imposed on innocent others. How excruciatingly painful to all involved when a choice to drink and drive results in the death of both innocent and not-so-innocent loved ones.

Whether our anguish comes from our own misjudgments or

the misjudgments of others, when we think that life isn't fair and we're ready to throw in the towel, we need to remind ourselves of the beautiful "Aha!" message of the gospel. *In the face of exasperating uncertainty,* grace *turns the outcome in our favor.* Thus, it is not only desirable but rational to have *hope* in the face of uncertainty. When dealing with adversity, the ups and downs and "vicissitudes of life," it is perfectly *rational* for us to encourage our hopes and not our fears. In truth, we need fear neither justice nor uncertainty. We have one amazing advantage—the grace of God!

But what exactly is this grace of which we speak? We can best understand what grace is and how it spreads its wide umbrella to protect us from the two irrevocables, the heat of justice and the wind and rain of uncertainty, by reviewing some basic principles of the plan of redemption.

GRACE: BACK TO BASICS

The overall logic for God's plan of salvation for his children goes essentially like this:

1. The goal or desired result of God's plan is to have his children become like him by obtaining a physical body, gaining knowledge, developing a Godly character, and developing wisdom and judgment.

2. Developing character, wisdom, and judgment requires moral agency.

3. Moral agency involves the concepts of right and wrong, good and bad, opposition in all things, and, therefore,

consequences in the form of punishments and rewards (i.e., a system of justice and justification).

4. Moral agency also implies uncertainty because if every outcome is certain, there is no meaning to agency and no development of wisdom and judgment.

5. If uncertainty and agency are necessary conditions for growth and development, and if maximum participation in Heavenly Father's plan is desired, then the plan must include a mechanism that will:

    a. promote a climate of learning;

    b. encourage wise risk taking;

    c. minimize the eternal consequences of mistakes made while learning, for those who are sincere;

    d. minimize the completion time required, consistent with other provisions.

God is perfectly just and believes in exactness in his accounting; therefore, every law is accompanied by a penalty for noncompliance. But the exact imposition of penalties could constitute a major deterrent to participation in the plan, particularly in light of the uncertainty in the trial and error process that characterizes growth toward perfection. (Remember the man with the single talent in the parable.) We know God loves his children and wishes to encourage the process of perfection; and he embodies the divine and perfected trait of mercy. Therefore, he provided in his plan (variously referred to as the plan of redemption, plan of happiness, and plan of salvation) a mechanism acknowledging agency but also allowing the demands of justice to be met without the extensive individual suffering that would otherwise be the case. This mechanism is essential to the process of redemption because it allows for penalties to be paid and for suffering to be endured by a designated surrogate or substitute party. The plan also allows for the specification of a set of conditions that must be met for the substitution to be valid or in force. In addition, the plan requires the surrogate to actually experience the penalties in order for his suffering to satisfy the demands of justice.

The conditions set and extended by the surrogate (or by God himself) may be thought of as the "cost" or "price" to the petitioner. For example, the penalties could be discounted by a set amount—say 50 percent, or 90 percent. In such a penalty-sharing case, the petitioner would pay only 50 percent or 10 percent of the penalty, and the balance would be paid by the surrogate. Or perhaps the surrogate might pay 100 percent of the penalty and request some other form of acknowledgement from the petitioner (such as a broken heart, a contrite spirit, and restitution). In this case, the part of the penalty paid by the surrogate would be characterized as a favor, clemency, or gift. In fact, this is the plan that was adopted. In great love, the surrogate paid 100 percent of the penalty for our sins and errors, requiring of us in return a broken heart.

Did such a provision for surrogate suffering absolutely have to be included in the plan? It could be argued that God could have suppressed his divine trait of mercy and focused only on justice. He conceivably could have taken the position that coming to a justified and perfected state is hard work and should therefore require endless time and suffering. Some intrepid souls may still have concluded that godhood was worth the risk of personal suffering without any provision for relief and still have carried on in the plan. God's work and glory, to bring to pass the immortality and eternal life of man, could conceivably still have been fulfilled, but perhaps for only a very few souls.

But the issue is moot, for Alma instructs us that "the work of justice could not be destroyed; if so, God would cease to be God" (Alma 42:13). The same claim can undoubtably be made for mercy. Without it God would cease to be God. Just as important, in *Lectures on Faith* Joseph Smith listed the attributes of godliness that enable us to exercise faith in God. Included are his justice, his mercy, and his love! (*Lectures on Faith*, Salt Lake City: Deseret Book Co., 1985, 3:20, 24; 4:13, 15). The implication is that our willingness to have faith in the plan is inextricably entwined with our knowledge of God's divine attributes.

Thus God in his mercy *gave* to his children a provision that would allow a surrogate to suffer, that the demands of justice might be met. God *gave* his Only Begotten Son, Jesus Christ, to be the surrogate and also gave him *power* he could exercise on behalf of those meeting the specified conditions. The power to overcome physical death, as well as spiritual death is God's *gift* to those who meet the proper conditions. These blessings flow from God's *love* for his children and his desire to watch over and *protect* them from the ultimate effects of sin.

The plan, then, includes at least the following elements:

1. *Love* of God for his children.

2. The *favor* or *gift* from God of a provision establishing a surrogate.

3. God's *gift* of his Beloved Son to be the surrogate.

4. Conveyance of *power* to Christ as the surrogate.

5. *Love* of Christ for the Father's children.

6. Christ's *gift* of his own life.

7. Conditional *clemency* from Christ to the petitioners—us.

8. *Forgiveness* of Adam's transgression as part of the clemency.

9. Extension of enabling *power* from Christ to eligible petitioners.

10. *Protection* from sin (through the shield of faith, prayer, and so forth).

We can see that encompassed in the plan are the important concepts of *love* (both from the Father and the Son), *favor, gifts* (again both from the Father and the Son), *power, clemency,* and *protection.* It appears that the word *grace as found in the scriptures may be thought of as an umbrella word designed to capture one or more of these concepts in the plan of redemption, depending on the context and emphasis desired by the writer or translator.*

To illustrate the notion that love, favor, gifts, power, clemency, and protection could all be included under the umbrella word *grace,* consider the following passages of scripture (with emphasis added). The parenthetical words are my own interpretation of what might be meant in each passage; other meanings might also be legitimate, and there may be even more overlap than indicated. For instance, it may be that *divine love* is an element of each of the scriptures below.

Genesis 6:8: "Noah found *grace* in the eyes of the Lord" (divine love, favor).

Luke 2:40: "And the child grew, and waxed strong in spirit, filled with wisdom: and the *grace* of God was upon him" (divine love, favor, protection).

Acts 4:33: "And with great power gave the apostles witness of the resurrection of the Lord Jesus: and great *grace* was upon them all" (divine favor).

Acts 15:11: "But we believe that through the *grace* of the Lord Jesus Christ we shall be saved, even as they" (gift, enabling power).

2 Nephi 10:24: "After ye are reconciled unto God, . . . it is only in and through the *grace* of God that ye are saved" (enabling power).

2 Nephi 11:5: "And also my soul delighteth in the covenants of the Lord which he hath made to our fathers; yea, my soul delighteth in his *grace*, and in his justice, and power, and mercy in the great and eternal plan of deliverance from death" (enabling power, divine love, protection).

Jacob 4:7: "Nevertheless, the Lord God showeth us our weakness that we may know that it is by his *grace*, and his great condescensions unto the children of men, that we have power to do these things" (enabling power, unmerited gift, disposition to be loving, generous, helpful).

Mosiah 18:16: "They were baptized in the waters of Mormon, and were filled with the *grace* of God" (divine love).

D&C 20:32: "But there is a possibility that man may fall from *grace* and depart from the living God" (divine favor).

D&C 138:14: "All these had departed the mortal life, firm in the hope of a glorious resurrection, through the *grace* of God the Father and his Only Begotten Son, Jesus Christ" (love, divine favor, enabling power of both the Father and the Son).

These are but a few of the many passages found throughout the scriptures that illustrate how *grace* can have multiple meanings. All these scriptural meanings are derived from the features that the Father and the Son incorporated into the plan of redemption.

GRACE AND PRECIOUS TRUTHS

In the concept of *grace* we see an example of plain and precious truths that have been taken from the scriptures. Scribes and translators without the benefit of correct principles or the gift of the Holy Ghost struggled to convey meaning and chose a word with broad interpretation when they couldn't be more definitive. A good illustration might be Acts 15:11, which reads, "But we believe that through the *grace* of the Lord Jesus Christ we shall be saved, even as they" (emphasis added). Here is an example where we as Latter-day Saints might be inclined to replace the word *grace* (meaning here, as stated above, a gift of enabling power) with *atonement*. Thus the passage could read, "But we believe that through the *atonement* of the Lord Jesus Christ we shall be saved, even as they." This has a familiar ring, of course, because as precious truths and meanings were restored to the Prophet Joseph Smith, he chose to render the concept as "We believe that *through the Atonement of Christ*, all mankind may be saved, by obedience to the laws and ordinances of the Gospel" (Articles of Faith 1:3). The replacement of the word *grace* with *atonement* is a very interesting notion we will explore further later.

As Latter-day Saints we have the wonderful advantage of restored truths and insights. We understand the plan of redemption and the role of Christ in that plan; as a result, our vocabulary is enriched immensely. We know how *love, favor, gift, power, clemency, protection,* and other, similar words describe various features of the plan.

It is easy to see why the term *grace* can be used so broadly and have many possible meanings. A writer who wishes to convey the love of God, his divine favor and protection, the power of the atonement, the gift of his Son, clemency, and mercy may choose to encapsulate all these concepts together in a single word. This approach would be especially useful if a writer or translator has an imperfect understanding of Christ and his mission and wished to communicate that a loving God had done something for man that was difficult to define. All of what God had done or would do that is imperfectly understood could be conveniently referenced as "the grace of God."

GRACE AS POWER

While there are a number of possible interpretations of the word *grace*, perhaps the substance of the word as it is commonly used can best be captured by thinking of grace as *an enabling power or divine means of help or strength.* In fact, there are some interesting insights to be gained by exploring the idea that grace is an enabling power.

One of the provisions of the plan of redemption is for God the Father to give power to his Son and in turn for the Son to extend that power to those who meet the required conditions. We read in Helaman, "He [Christ] hath *power* given unto him from the Father to redeem them from their sins because of repentance" (Helaman 5:11; emphasis added). This verse points out clearly that Christ is given power from his Father. Further, in the Doctrine and Covenants we read that Christ will in turn give that power to those who receive him, "But verily, verily, I say unto you, that as many as receive me, to them will I give *power* to become the sons of God, even to them that believe on my name" (D&C 11:30; emphasis added).

It appears to be this bestowal of *power*—or *enabling power*—that Nephi views as a significant aspect of grace. In 2 Nephi 10:24 we read, "Wherefore, my beloved brethren, reconcile yourselves to the will of God, and not to the will of the devil and the flesh; and remember, after ye are reconciled unto God, that it is only in and through the *grace* of God that ye are saved. Wherefore, may God raise you from death by the *power* of the resurrection, and also from everlasting death by the *power* of the atonement, . . . that ye may praise him through grace divine" (emphasis added).

The interpretation of grace as enabling power has much to recommend it. In his article, "Grace as Power," biblical scholar John Nolland writes about the Greek word χάρις, which is the word often translated as grace. He observes that a number of scholars agree that this word denotes "a substantial power streaming down from the divine world." Nolland continues, "The word is seen to designate a tangible power at work in the believer. The semantic conditions for such a use are already met in the usage of both classical Greek and the Jewish Greek of the diaspora" (John Nolland, "Grace as Power," in *Novum Testimentum* 28, no. 1 [1986]: 26–27). Nolland is arguing that the Greek word χάρις, which is often translated as *grace*, could appropriately be translated as *power* and that the origins of that meaning of the word can be traced as far back as the scattering of the tribes of Israel.

To see how useful it is to have an alternative and insightful translation of the Greek, consider a fascinating example from Luke 4: "And he came to Nazareth, where he had been brought up: and as his custom was, he went into the synagogue on the sabbath day, and stood up for to read. And there was delivered unto him the book of the prophet Esaias. And when he had opened the book, he found the place where it was written,

"The Spirit of the Lord is upon me, because he hath anointed me to preach the gospel to the poor; he hath sent me to heal the brokenhearted, to preach deliverance to the captives, and recovering of sight to the blind, to set at liberty them that are bruised, to preach the acceptable year of the Lord.

"And he closed the book, and he gave it again to the minister, and sat down. And the eyes of all them that were in the synagogue were fastened on him. And he began to say unto them, This day is this scripture fulfilled in your ears. And all bare him witness, and wondered at the *gracious* words which proceeded out of his mouth. And they said, Is not this Joseph's son?" (Luke 4:16–22; emphasis added).

In verse 22, Luke seems to indicate that Jesus' words were apparently received positively. At least that is the inference we would make from the description of Jesus' words as *gracious*. But several verses later, in Luke 4:28–29, we read:

"And all they in the synagogue, when they heard these things, were filled with wrath, and rose up, and thrust him out of the city, and led him unto the brow of the hill whereon their city was built, that they might cast him down headlong."

John Nolland suggests that the explanation of this rapid transition from seeming acceptance to rejection has eluded scholars due to a mistranslation of the original Greek. When the Greek is inappropriately translated as "gracious" (or "winsome" or "pleasing," as some have suggested), we are naturally led to wonder what may have evoked the subsequent sudden change of attitude of those in the synagogue. But according to Nolland, in Luke 4:22 the Greek word χάρις that is translated "gracious words" could have more accurately been rendered as "words of God's grace." This translation fits the preceding verses better, where Jesus speaks of preaching the gospel, healing the brokenhearted, and preaching deliverance to the captives. These are better understood as words of God's grace, or *power*, than as "gracious"—or pleasing—words. This translation then explains why in subsequent verses the people of the synagogue expressed their wrath.

It is misleading to think that those in the synagogue had a sudden change of mind. A better rendering of the original

Greek allows us to understand that the people viewed Jesus as a pretender to God's grace or power and were thereby greatly offended.* Furthermore, another scholar, Joachim Jeremias, argues that there was no change in the attitude of the hearers throughout the course of the incident. From the outset, their response was unanimous rage to the message of Jesus. This viewpoint comes from interpreting the original Greek in verse 22 *not* as "all bare him witness" but rather as "they bore witness against him" (*Jesus' Promise to the Nations*, Naperville, Ill.: A. R. Allenson, 1958, 44–46).

From this example, we can see how scribes and translators could either intentionally or ignorantly alter meanings intended by the original writer. *In this case, as in most others, the alteration is biased in the direction of diminishing the role and influence of Christ.* Nephi had it right. We are saved from death and hell by the atoning *power* of Christ (2 Nephi 10:25). The *willingness and ability* of Christ to use that power on our behalf (subject to conditions of repentance) is the essence of the grace of Jesus Christ.

The Book of Mormon prophet Jacob directly equates grace with power: "Our faith becometh unshaken, insomuch that we truly can command in the name of Jesus and the very trees obey us, or the mountains, or the waves of the sea. Nevertheless, the Lord God showeth us our weakness that we may know that it is

---

*A. Loisy explains it as "On avrait été frappé de sa prétention plus que du charme de sa parole" (*Les Evangiles Synoptiques* 1 [Montier-en-Der, 1907]: 844). Translation of the French means "one would have been struck by his pretension more than by his charming [gracious] words" (translation by S. Nadauld).

by his *grace*, and his great condescensions unto the children of men that we have *power* to do these things" (Jacob 4:6–7; emphasis added).

GRACE AND ATONEMENT

We may wonder about the modest aversion to the word *grace* that seems to prevail in our Latter-day Saint culture. One quite legitimate reason could come from the religious tradition that salvation comes only through grace, without regard to personal works. Because we know this view to be incomplete at best and simply wrong at worst, we might be persuaded to maintain some distance from the concept of grace in the name of doctrinal purity.

But I believe there is another much more interesting and potentially insightful phenomenon at work here. Consider this: The LDS Topical Guide provides more than fifty references to the word *grace* scattered throughout the Old and New Testaments. However, the same Topical Guide contains only two biblical references to the word *atonement* (see "Jesus Christ, Atonement through"; the references are Leviticus 17:11 and Romans 5:11). In fact, the word *atonement* is used only once in the entire New Testament (Romans 5:11). On the other hand, the Book of Mormon index contains more than twenty references to the word *atonement*, in addition to a like number of references to the word *grace*. What are we to make of this? I believe a good case can be made for the notion that, at least to a degree, when we say *atonement*, they (i.e., others in the Christian world) say *grace*.

Before the coming forth of the Book of Mormon, the religious vocabulary of Christians could come only from the Bible. And we have learned that, unfortunately, "many plain and precious" truths were taken from the Bible; as Nephi taught, "because of the many plain and precious things which have been taken out of the book, . . . an exceedingly great many do stumble" (1 Nephi 13:29). But we have been blessed in our day with the Book of Mormon, whose announced purpose is to be another witness of Jesus Christ. Part of that witnessing process is to provide a better understanding of his mission—and an enhanced vocabulary for expressing the true points of his doctrine. Thus we can speak with clarity and specificity of the atoning sacrifice of Christ, which he wrought in the Garden of Gethsemane and on the cross at Calvary. From the Book of Mormon we understand the purpose of the atonement and its infinite reach in detail and are not left to ponder on the biblical interpretation of grace and what might lie under its broad umbrella.

With that in mind, it is important that we not be put off by the term *grace* because of some doctrine we might believe the word implies. We would presumably be just as much in error to state that we are "saved" by the *atonement alone* as we would be to say we are saved by *grace alone*. We have clearly seen from our study of justification that works do matter. Furthermore, we know that grace cannot be abused; the Holy Ghost must ensure that the atoning blood of Christ is applied only to those who have honestly and completely met the conditions for its application. Therefore, because the concept of grace encompasses the love, favor, protection, and power of God and Christ, *all of which we believe in fervently,* and because we understand it cannot be abused in its application or confused relative to works, we ought to encourage its proper use. Our enhanced understanding of the plain and precious truths of the gospel should enable us to embrace with equal enthusiasm both the atonement and grace when each is used in the correct context and with the correct meaning.

GRACIOUS LIVING

Gracious living does not mean living à la Martha Stewart. In actuality, the root word of *gracious* is *grace.* Thus, "gracious living" means living in acknowledgment of the grace of God. It means living without fear of justice or being anxious over uncertainty and therefore living unhurried, untrammeled, and unafraid. It promotes an attitude of love and forgiveness because we are loved and can be forgiven. It is living as a conduit, with the grace of God flowing in to us from heaven and out from us to our fellow man. Graciousness is an attitude toward others stemming from our recognition that, having received grace from the Savior, we should extend it to others. One who is gracious is kind, forgiving, and makes others feel at ease. Graciousness is a comeliness in form, demeanor, attitude, and speech that signals acceptance of self and others.

By contrast, William H. Poteat suggests, "Human existence is the very opposite of graceful. It is awkward—which is to say, it is 'turning-the-wrong-way-ward!'" ("On the Meaning of Grace," *The Hibbert Journal* 57 [1958]: 156). When we turn to ourselves we are turning the wrong way. The angst and awkwardness of modern society is reflected in the plethora of self-help books, the extensive use of mind-numbing drugs, the hours spent in psychiatric counseling, and the allure of horoscopes, tarot cards, and psychics.

This "turning-the-wrong-way-ward" notion is captured beautifully in the first section of the Doctrine and Covenants, which was given as the Lord's preface to the doctrines revealed in this dispensation. In verse 16 the Lord says of us, "They seek not the Lord to establish his righteousness, but every man walketh in his own way, and after the image of his own god, whose image is in the likeness of the world" (D&C 1:16).

Every man walking "in his own way" and "after the image of his own God" is certainly a turning-the-wrong-way-ward, grace-less, awkward way of life; it is a clear description of the conditions that prompted the Lord to call a prophet and reveal truths anew from heaven. The Prophet Joseph Smith was to proclaim the revealed truth, "Man should not counsel his fellow man, neither trust in the arm of flesh—but that every man might speak in the name of God the Lord, even the Savior of the world" (D&C 1:19–20).

Speaking in the name of the Lord and acknowledging his power, love, and mercy—his grace—is an antidote to turning-the-wrong-way-wardness and is the essence of gracious living. Sincerely acknowledging the grace of God eliminates pride, that ungraceful, turning-the-wrong-way-ward trait that prevents us from accessing the blessings of the atonement.

A gracious approach to life—one that acknowledges our

weaknesses and reliance on the Savior for forgiveness—is a significant stimulus to our personal growth as well as the growth of others. In a religious context, we have observed that the exactness of justification and the allowance for learning through trial and error promotes optimal personal growth. An interesting and revealing parallel can be observed in a secular setting. The very popular book of some years ago titled *In Search of Excellence* (Thomas J. Peters and Robert H. Waterman Jr., New York: Bantam Books, 1982) described characteristics of top performing business organizations. One element common to all excellent organizations was described as the principle of "tight-loose." Those organizations whose outcome measures were ranked the highest and whose people consistently exhibited the highest performance had a "tight-loose" work environment. Standards and expectations for revenues, costs, net income, productivity, and product development were well-defined and *tight*. But individuals were allowed a wide latitude in how they went about meeting the standards. *Loose* innovation and creativity were promoted. If one made an honest effort, failure was allowed, and changing behavior was encouraged and applauded.

We should not be surprised that the conditions of exacting standards and individual agency, conditions deemed optimal by our Heavenly Father for growth in this mortal state, would also have been discovered by business organizations as those conditions that promote optimal performance.

THE GRACE OF GOD AND THE GRACE OF CHRIST

The essence of the *grace of God,* meaning the Father, is his willingness or disposition to provide a way for his children to progress more quickly and successfully through the conditions that promote optimal growth, including justice and uncertainty. Thus we may think of grace as a divine means of help or strength or as an enabling power. We are enabled to overcome sin by repenting and calling upon the atonement of Christ to meet the demands of justice. We are empowered to overcome physical death by that same atonement, which brings about the resurrection of all who will die. We know that God gave his Son power to make intercession for men (2 Nephi 2:9; Mosiah 14:12; 15:8).

The essence of the *grace of Christ* is his willingness to use his power and influence on our behalf. We know the Lord pleads the cause of his people (2 Nephi 8:22; 13:13). He himself has said, "Lift up your hearts and be glad, for I am in your midst, and am your advocate with the Father" (D&C 29:5). It is his influence and light that gives life to all things, enlightens our eyes, and quickens our understanding (D&C 88:11, 13). It is by the power granted to him by the Father and extended to us that we will overcome both physical and spiritual death. Nephi admonishes us, "Wherefore, may God raise you from death by the power of the resurrection, and also from everlasting death by the power of the atonement, that ye may be received into the eternal kingdom of God, that ye may praise him through *grace divine*" (2 Nephi 10:25; emphasis added).

Thus the grace of God—as represented by his love for his children, the gift of his Son, and the Son's atoning sacrifice—provides a way for us to overcome the demands of justice and more quickly return to our Father's presence.

If the grace of God and Christ were focused only on the demands of justice it would be amazing enough. But there is more! We may call upon the grace of Christ to ease the pain and anxiety that comes from living in a world of difficult choices and uncertain outcomes. The Savior invites us to "come unto me, all ye that labour and are heavy laden, and I will give you rest. Take my yoke upon you, and learn of me: for I am meek and lowly in heart: and ye shall find rest unto your souls" (Matthew 11:28–29). Further, we are taught, "He shall go forth, suffering pains and afflictions and temptations of every kind; and this that the word might be fulfilled which saith he will take upon him the pains and the sicknesses of his people. . . . And he will take upon him their infirmities, that his bowels may be filled with mercy, according to the flesh, that he may know according to the flesh how to succor his people according to their infirmities" (Alma 7:11–12). When we are visited by death or illness or disappointment, whether by our own poor choices or the choices of others, we may know that the Savior understands and knows "how to succor his people according to their infirmities."

Katharina von Schlegel beautifully captures the notion of the Savior's grace in the face of our uncertainty:

> Be still, my soul: The Lord is on thy side;
> With patience bear thy cross of grief or pain.

Leave to thy God to order and provide;
In ev'ry change he faithful will remain.
Be still, my soul: Thy best, thy heav'nly Friend
Thru thorny ways leads to a joyful end.

Be still, my soul: Thy God doth undertake
To guide the future as he has the past.
Thy hope, thy confidence let nothing shake;
All now mysterious shall be bright at last.
Be still, my soul: The waves and winds still know
His voice who ruled them while he dwelt below.

Be still, my soul: The hour is hast'ning on
When we shall be forever with the Lord,
When disappointment, grief, and fear are gone,
Sorrow forgot, love's purest joys restored.
Be still, my soul: When change and tears are past,
All safe and blessed we shall meet at last.
(*Hymns*, no. 124.)

AMAZING GRACE, A SONG OF REDEEMING LOVE

Consider this beautiful vignette played out in the Book of Mormon. In Alma 5, Alma the Younger has given up the judgment seat but retained the office of high priest, and he has undertaken the task of preaching the word of God unto the people. Beginning in the city of Zarahemla, he invites the people to remember that his father, Alma the Elder, "preached the word unto your fathers, and a mighty change was also wrought in their hearts, and they humbled themselves and put their trust in the true and living God. And behold, they were faithful until the end: therefore they were saved" (Alma 5:13).

Alma asks the people if they themselves have experienced this mighty change in their hearts and if they would feel confident standing in the presence of their God. He continues by asking, "If ye have experienced a change of heart, and if ye have felt to sing the song of redeeming love, I would ask, can ye feel so now?" (Alma 5:26). Alma may have been using the phrase "sing a song of redeeming love" in a figurative way, or perhaps there was an actual song whose words he was evoking to touch the hearts of his listeners. In our day we are blessed with a number of songs that express the redeeming love of the Savior, but few are more powerful in melody or moving in words than the song "Amazing Grace."

It is amazing to be *loved* by God and his Son. It is amazing to be *protected* from the ultimate effects of sin because of that love, which led to the atoning sacrifice of Christ. It is amazing to receive the *enabling power* that comes from the Savior if we will but receive him and come to repentance with a broken heart and contrite spirit. Truly, his grace is amazing.

The redeeming love of the Savior is *amazing*. The scriptures tell us that when the Savior appeared at the temple in the land of Bountiful, the people were so amazed that "the whole multitude fell to the earth; for they remembered that it had been prophesied among them that Christ should show himself unto them after his ascension into heaven" (3 Nephi 11:12). No doubt the physical presence of the Lord and the drama of his appearance were amazing, but I believe the people's response was evoked just as much by the deep understanding they had of his mission as Savior and Redeemer as by the drama.

Nephi, who led the Lord's people at this time, was a great-great-grandson of Alma the Elder, who had been converted by Abinadi and who baptized at the waters of Mormon (Mosiah 17–18). It was Abinadi who had been challenged by the priests of King Noah as they said to him, "What meaneth the words which are written, and which have been taught by our fathers saying: How beautiful upon the mountains are *the feet of him* that bringeth good tidings: that publisheth peace; that bringeth good tidings of good; that publisheth salvation; that saith unto Zion, Thy God reigneth" (Mosiah 12:20–21).

It was Abinadi's explanation of these words that led to the conversion of Alma and that later led Alma the Younger to invite the people of his day to remember the mighty change that had been wrought in their hearts. I believe Abinadi's teachings of "beautiful feet" bringing salvation and grace were passed from father to son, from Alma the Elder to Alma the Younger, then to the older Helaman and the younger Helaman, and finally down to Nephi and his son, Nephi. And I believe this final Nephi must have treasured up in his heart the teachings of the beautiful feet bringing salvation and had shared them with the people.

This seems evident to me because the scriptures record a very tender scene that was played out as part of the Savior's initial appearance to the Nephites. After the people had come forth one by one to witness the resurrected Christ for themselves, "it came to pass that he spake unto Nephi (for Nephi was among the multitude) and he commanded him that he should come forth. And Nephi arose and went forth, and bowed himself before the Lord and did *kiss his feet*" (3 Nephi 11:18–19; emphasis added). Nephi had been taught about the beautiful feet bringing salvation, and when he found himself in the presence of the Savior his response of gratitude and love was to kneel and kiss his feet.

Each of us will also one day be in the presence of God. Alma describes the possibilities: "Do ye exercise faith in the redemption of him who created you? Do you look forward with an eye of faith, and view this mortal body raised in immortality, and this corruption raised in incorruption, to stand before God to be judged according to the deeds which have been done in the mortal body?

"I say unto you, can you imagine to yourselves that ye hear the voice of the Lord, saying unto you, in that day: Come unto me ye blessed, for behold, your works have been the works of righteousness upon the face of the earth? . . . Or otherwise, can ye imagine yourselves brought before the tribunal of God with your souls filled with guilt and remorse, having a remembrance of all your guilt, yea, a perfect remembrance of all your wickedness, yea, a remembrance that ye have set at defiance the commandments of God? . . .

"I say unto you, ye will know at that day that ye cannot be saved; for there can no man be saved except his garments are washed white; yea, his garments must be purified until they are cleansed from all stain, through the blood of him of whom it has been spoken by our fathers, who should come to redeem his people from their sins" (Alma 5:15–16, 18, 21).

Our knowledge of the truthfulness of the statement that "there can no man be saved except his garments are washed white . . . through the blood of him of whom it has been spoken by our fathers, who should come to redeem his people from their sins" should cause each of us to wish in that day to kneel and kiss the feet of the Savior whose blood was shed for our individual sins.

Surely our song of redeeming love could be "Amazing Grace."

> Amazing grace! How sweet the sound
> That saved a wretch like me.
> I once was lost but now am found,
> was blind, but now I see.
>
> 'Twas grace that taught my heart to fear
> and grace my fears relieved.
> How precious did that grace appear
> The hour I first believed!

THE INTERRELATIONSHIP OF FAITH, JUSTIFICATION, AND GRACE

Faith, justification, and grace are three concepts central to Christian theology. The understanding of these three concepts for Latter-day Saints rests on the foundation principle that we are children of a Heavenly Father who wishes to have us become like him and return to his presence. To that end, God the Father has instituted laws (or commandments) and associated penalties. We must keep the law or pay the penalty associated with the broken law. Justification is the process by which it is determined whether or not we have kept the laws with exactness. The penalty for a broken law may be avoided by understanding that God has provided for us a Savior, his son, Jesus Christ, who has atoned for our sins upon condition of repentance. If we have faith in Jesus Christ, if we believe he has atoned for our sins and are willing on the basis of that belief to repent, then we can meet the demands of the law through Jesus Christ, or be justified by our faith in him. If we choose not to exercise faith in Christ, we will be left to meet the demands of justice through our own suffering.

Thus our faith in Christ allows us to be justified without the personal suffering that would otherwise be the case. That is why it is so very important that we develop our faith in Christ to the point that we are motivated to acknowledge him as our Savior and Redeemer and seek the mighty change of heart spoken of in the scriptures.

If we have faith in Christ, if we desire to be justified by repenting and forsaking our sins, then we are promised that through the power of the atonement, or by the grace of God, we will be forgiven of our sins and cleansed by the blood of Christ. In other words, our faith in Christ allows us to be justified to God's exacting standard by taking advantage of the atoning sacrifice of Christ. This possibility for justification is available to us through the grace of God the Father, as well as the grace of his son, Jesus Christ.

Thus faith, justification, and grace are woven together in a beautiful fabric whose intent is to wrap us in God's love and convey us home again to him.

CONCLUSION

I believe the principles of the gospel are remarkable in their simplicity and compelling in their logic. I also believe the better they are understood, the more they will be appreciated and hopefully the more they will be lived. Each of the three principles dealt with in this book works together to bless our lives immeasurably.

We cannot live on the earth and learn the lessons our Father in Heaven intended without understanding faith and making it a guiding principle in our lives. The benefits of developing faith make its pursuit worthy of our most rigorous intellectual and spiritual efforts. I hope the definition we have developed makes it possible for everyone to better understand faith and to realize how it may be increased.

What a blessing to know that though faith is an intangible principle, it is not mystical or undefinable. We have learned that having faith means accepting assurances and evidences that Christ is indeed the Son of God and that the promises of a glorious resurrection and eternal life are rational expectations. Those who have not listened to the assurances, have not sifted and weighed the evidence, or have perfunctorily dismissed the issue as trivial will forfeit the most extraordinary blessings.

Those extraordinary blessings that come from faith are linked to two conditions that operate to insure our optimal growth and development in this mortal sphere. Both conditions are required for us to develop the wisdom and judgment necessary to become like our Heavenly Father. The first condition is the establishment of a set of laws and consequences, or a system of justice. The second condition is the existence of agency and uncertainty.

To learn how faith is related to justice, we have had to gain a better understanding of the principle of justification. Justification is achieved when we satisfy the demands of justice in one or more of three possible ways: First, by obeying the law; second, by having Christ pay the penalty, subject to specified conditions; and third, by our personally suffering the consequences for breaking the law. We have learned that the Holy Ghost is responsible for monitoring the justification process and certifying that the atoning blood of Christ is applied only when warranted.

Since the learning process involves trial and error for every mortal except Christ, we will each have to suffer punishment for sins unless the extraordinary blessings of the atonement are sought and received. Only those who believe in Christ and fulfill his requirements will be forgiven and avoid the personal sufferings that justice would otherwise require. Thus faith in Christ provides the most wonderful of blessings—forgiveness of sins and justification through the surrogate suffering of the Savior.

Another extraordinary blessing is linked to the condition of agency, or uncertainty. Things happen that we have no control over. Accidents, sicknesses, disappointments, heartaches, and troubles are an integral part of our mortal experience. But the Savior invites us to take his yoke upon us and learn of him, for his yoke is easy and his burden is light, and by learning of him we will find rest unto our souls (Matthew 11:28–30). He has offered to take upon him our pains and sicknesses that we may be supported and sustained in times of trial and heartache (Alma 7:11–13; 36:3).

Thus, as we journey through life we are supported by the love, favor, compassion, and empowerment of God and his Son. The love of God, the gift of his Son, and the power to return to live with them constitute the grace that weighs the outcomes of this mortal experience in our favor. Truly "amazing grace" may be our song of redeeming love.

If we develop faith, if we exercise faith by repenting and becoming justified through the atonement of Christ, if we seek his grace and live according to his word, we shall surely be blessed to kneel and kiss his feet and acknowledge him as our Savior and Redeemer. Then we will be lifted up and invited to enter his kingdom, and there we and our loved ones may dwell forever with him in love and peace.

This is the doctrine expounded by the now familiar scripture, "Therefore being justified by faith, we have peace with God through our Lord Jesus Christ: By whom also we have access by faith into this grace wherein we stand and rejoice in hope of the glory of God" (Romans 5:1–2). This is our hope, our desire, our earnest expectation, born of an understanding of faith, justification, and grace. I believe these things with all my heart. I stand and rejoice in hope of the glory of God, and pray that we may each be so blessed.

Index

Adam, as recipient of heavenly assurances, 25–27

"Amazing Grace," 122, 151, 154

Angels: as sources of heavenly assurances, 23–24, 26, 28–29; duties of, 24

Apostles and prophets, as sources of mortal assurances, 21–22

Assurances, heavenly: vs. mortal assurances, 10; need for, 22–23; role of, 23, 24–25; angels as sources of, 23–24, 26, 28–29; Holy Ghost as source of, 25, 26, 27, 29–30; God as source of, 25–26, 28; Adam as recipient of, 25–27; Joseph Smith as recipient of, 28–30; in combination with mortal assurances, 30–32. *See also* Faith and heavenly assurances

Assurances, mortal: as the starting point for developing faith, 10; vs. heavenly assurances, 10; parents as sources of, 10–12; fast-and-testimony meetings as sources of, 12–13; Alma's teachings to the Zoramites as, 13–15; compared to a seed, 14–15, 72–74; importance to missionary work, 15–16; prophets and apostles as sources of, 21–22; local Church leaders as sources of, 22; as preparation for heavenly assurances, 24–25; in combination with heavenly assurances, 30–32. *See also* Faith and mortal assurances

Atonement: satisfying the law through repentance and, 91–93, 95–96, 97–98, 100; and grace, 143–45

Balloon, lifting power of faith compared to helium, 1–2

Baptism: observing the ordinance of, 84; dealing with past compliance problems through, 86–87

Bible: importance of, 41–42; as macroevidence, 41–42; power of, 42

Book of Mormon: as macroevidence, 42–43; purpose of, 42–43; power of, 43

Celestial glory: conditions of those inheriting, 110; outcomes for those inheriting, 110–11; characterized by complete acceptance of Christ and the Holy Ghost, 111–12; and the resurrection, 112; summary of characteristics of those inheriting, 116–17

Church leaders, as sources of mortal assurances, 21–22

Compliance officers: in the secular world, 82–83; Holy Ghost as a "compliance officer," 83–86, 104–5

Cowley, Matthew, 4

Creation of the world: as macroevidence, 36–40; science vs. religion on, 38–40

Death, faith as an operative principle after, 20–21

Diagnosing faith, 54–56

Doctrine and Covenants, as
macroevidence, 44

Event evidence: Nephi's (son of Lehi)
use of, 44–46; Alma's use of, 46;
Nephi's (son of Helaman) use of,
46–47; latter-day occurrences as, 47
Evidence: experience of boy
vacationing in Hawaii, 33–34;
acceptance of, as faith, 34–35. *See
also* Macroevidence; Microevidence
Exactness: in secular affairs, 78;
experience of Margaret Nadauld
giving babysitters instructions,
79–80; meeting the challenges of,
79–81; experience of elderly friend
with struggling brother, 80–81;
God's view of, 81–82
Exaltation, and justification, 105–7,
117–18, 120. *See also* Celestial glory

Faith: compared to a helium-filled
balloon, 1–2; difficulty of defining,
2; not constrained by lack of
understanding, 2; importance of
understanding, 2–3, 4–5;
experience with young couple
seeking to have children, 3–4;
experience of Matthew Cowley
with blind child, 4; as a religious
principle vs. other meanings, 5; as
substance or assurance, 6; Paul on,
6–8, 35; expanded definition of,
7–8, 32, 52–53; and things hoped
for, 8–9; seed of, 14–15, 72–74; as a
spiritual gift, 16–18; as a necessary
trait in the premortal existence,
18–20; as an operative principle
after death, 20–21; as the act of
accepting evidence, 34–35;
answering questions about,
53–54; diagnosing personal
faith, 54–55; diagnosing your
children's faith, 55–56; prescription
for investigator faith, 56–57;
prescription for rekindling faith, 57;

graphically plotting your personal
faith, 62–63, 65; blessing of, 76;
justification through, in Christ,
120–21; relationship to justification
and grace, 154–58. *See also*
Assurances, heavenly; Assurances,
mortal; Faith and heavenly
assurances; Faith and
macroevidence; Faith and
microevidence; Faith and mortal
assurances; Macroevidence;
Microevidence
Faith and heavenly assurances: graphs
depicting relationships between,
63–64, 70–73; conversion of Saul,
64–65; dramatic impact of spiritual
experiences, 64–65, 69, 71
Faith and macroevidence: graph
depicting relationship between, 66;
impact of personal vs. global
experiences, 67–68
Faith and microevidence: graph
depicting relationship between, 67;
impact of personal vs. global
experiences, 67–68
Faith and mortal assurances: inhibiting
the growth of faith, 60, 69;
enhancing the growth of faith,
60–61; graphs depicting
relationships between, 60–62,
70–73; "Doubting" Thomas, 61;
moving beyond mortal assurances
in developing faith, 71–75
Fast-and-testimony meetings, as
sources of mortal assurances, 12–13

Gifts, spiritual, 16–18
God: as the source of heavenly
assurances, 25–26, 28; grace of, 148
Grace: amazing nature of, 122–23,
150–54; and uncertainty, 123–24,
130–31; and understanding the
plan of salvation, 131–32; as a
mechanism satisfying the demands
of mercy and justice, 132–34;
multiple meanings of, 134–37; as an